John Ross Macduff

The Story of Jesus in Verse

Leading Incidents in the Great Biography

John Ross Macduff

The Story of Jesus in Verse
Leading Incidents in the Great Biography

ISBN/EAN: 9783337074531

Printed in Europe, USA, Canada, Australia, Japan

Cover: Foto ©ninafisch / pixelio.de

More available books at **www.hansebooks.com**

THE STORY OF JESUS

IN VERSE

Leading Incidents in the Great Biography

BY

J. R. MACDUFF D.D.

AUTHOR OF "MORNING AND NIGHT WATCHES" "MEMORIES OF BETHANY" ETC.

CASSELL AND COMPANY LIMITED
LONDON PARIS & MELBOURNE
1893

To

The Rev. GEORGE MATHESON

D.D. F.R.S.E.

ST. BERNARD'S EDINBURGH

THIS BOOK IS DEDICATED

WITH AFFECTION

AND IN ADMIRATION OF HIS GENIUS

PREFACE

THESE pages fulfil a long-cherished purpose,—to put into simple verse the more prominent incidents in our Lord's life. They have, *purposely*, in the higher and true sense of the word, no pretensions to "poetry," —poetry with subtle thought and recondite meaning. The idea is to give, as a versifier (no more), what might be termed a "rhythmic Harmony" of the Gospel story; in other words, an unambitious attempt to clothe the salient portions of the grandest of themes—"the true Song of Songs"—in a novel, and, as far as possible, pictorial shape. The writer has deemed it well to vary the versification, so as to avoid " monotonous uniformity"; indeed, leaving the pen very much to the impulse of the moment, while endeavouring at the same time to adapt style and measure to the incidents described. In some few cases, without using unwarrantable liberty with the sacred text, he has even adopted what may be called, for lack of a better term, the semi-dramatic form. Conscious of many shortcomings, he commends a somewhat bold but congenial task to the indulgence of his readers.

PROLOGUE

THE WORLD LONGING FOR THE ADVENT.

"*Watchman, what of the night? Watchman, what of the night? The morning cometh.*"—Isaiah xxi. 11, 12.

"*Unto you that fear My name shall the Sun of Righteousness arise with healing in His wings.*"—Malachi iv. 2.

Hear the cry of anguished nations
Sent despairing to the skies.
'Tis the baffled prayer of ages,
Uttered loud by seers and sages—
      Sun of Righteousness arise!

On the problem of salvation
Earth in vain all solvents tries.
Philosophy has failed to find them,
Seekers seek what only blinds them—
      Sun of Righteousness arise!

Four millenniums of "watchers"
Through the gloom had strained their eyes;
Long and anxiously they waited,
But they only cried belated—
      Sun of Righteousness arise!

He has come!—a world benighted
Answered has her yearning sighs
In God's own revealed Salvation!
Over every tribe and nation—
Sun of Righteousness arise!

"The dayspring from on high hath visited us: to give light to them that sit in darkness and in the shadow of death, to guide our feet into the way of peace."—Luke i. 78, 79.

LIST OF ILLUSTRATIONS.

NAZARETH ... ... *Frontispiece.*

PAGE

TRADITIONAL PLACE OF THE APPEARANCE TO THE
SHEPHERDS 2

THE JORDAN, NEAR THE DEAD SEA ... 16

NAIN 48

PLAIN OF GENNESARET 64

DISTANT VIEW OF MOUNT HERMON 68

VIEW FROM THE MOUNT OF OLIVES ... 80

GETHSEMANE 90

THE

Story of Jesus

IN VERSE.

I

[*Two travellers. A man leading an ass, on which a woman is seated. They meet an old countryman Scene: Slopes of the Mount of Olives.*]

"Tell us, tell us, where is Ephrath,
Home of Boaz, Ruth, and Jesse?
Thither for the great enrolment
We are speeding."

Countryman.—"Seek ye Bethlehem?
Bethlehem of the land of Judah—
That of which our prophet speaketh,*
As though least among its cities;
Yet from it shall come a Ruler
Who Jehovah's flock shall 'shepherd,'†
And whose name is 'Everlasting'?

* Micah v. 2.   † Lit. Hebrew.

B

See beyond the narrow valley
Where the stream of Kedron floweth:
See behind the Temple summits,
And the stately towers of Zion,
Gentle uplands crowned with olive !
Perched upon its rocky ridges:
That is Bethlehem !"

Travellers.—" Peace be with you ! "

Then the pilgrims, faint and weary,
Onward go in solemn silence.
Evening shadows fast were falling
As they crossed the ridge of Hinnom,
Toward the hoary tomb of Rachel.

Far across the mystic hollow
Gleamed the giant hills of Moab,
Every battlement transfigured
Into ruby, gold, and purple,
In the dying fires of sunset.

.   .   .   .   .

[*Scene : The Plains of Bethlehem.   Midnight.*]

Nature is hushed in stillness deep,
The birds with folded pinions sleep.
The stars their showers of lustre rain,
And silver all the silent plain.
When, lo ! a radiance strangely bright
Illuminates the vault of night,
The full-orbed heavenly splendour dies ;
And the new glory dims its brilliant galaxies.

TRADITIONAL PLACE OF THE APPEARANCE TO THE SHEPHERDS.

(To face p. 7.)

[*A group of Shepherds abiding in the Fields by Night.*]

* Hark! what midnight songs are these?
 Floateth whence this magic sound,
 As if celestial melodies
 Spread in concentric wavelets round?
 An Angel the glad tidings brings—
"THIS DAY TO YOU IS BORN THE KING OF KINGS!
 BY ALL THE HEAVENLY HOST ADORED,
 A SAVIOUR WHO IS CHRIST THE LORD."

. . . . .

Then suddenly a burst of song
In deepening echoes floats along.
Listen! the circling strains increase:
 They rise again—
"GLORY TO GOD, ON EARTH BE PEACE,
 GOOD WILL TO MEN!"

[*The Shepherds one to another.*]

"O brothers, let us haste to know
 What minstrel tidings these—
Sounding from Heaven to earth below
 In choral symphonies—
Glory to God! Good will to Men!
The dulcet echoes wake again?

O Thou, Great Shepherd of the sheep,
Thou who dost slumber not nor sleep,
Our trembling flocks in safety keep,—
While we mount the terraced vineyards,

* Luke ii. 8.

Girdling David's royal city,
Tell the message of the Angels,—
With the glorious sight we saw
From our fields of Ephratah!

. . . .

[*They journey on.*]

As the night dews were falling fast,
They hastened up the olive-slope.
Soon was the ancient gateway passed
In mingled awe, and joy, and hope.

Thence to the village inn they sped,
And, passing through the noisy throng,
They saw, laid on a manger-bed,
The child-God of the Angel-song.*

No "pomp of circumstance" or power,
No palace proud—no gilded hall,
Did homage in His natal hour,—
His cradle was that borrowed stall.

No troops of angels guarded Him.
Fed with a cruse of olive oil,
A lamp swung from the rafters dim.
His birthright poverty and toil.

There, in that fitful struggling light,
The Heavenly babe unconscious lay,
Mid yokes of oxen housed for night,
While wrangling traffic woke the day.

* Luke ii. 16.

Two lowly loving hearts alone
Kept vigil o'er the life begun :
Of low estate, they only own
A peasant home in Zebulon.

. . . .

Back to their flocks the Shepherds went
Filled with the honour done to them,
The first to hail the great event
Which consecrated BETHLEHEM ! *

* Luke ii. 20.

II

[An Eastern Caravan on the Way to Bethlehem.]

See, yet other heralds bring
Tribute to the infant King! *
Wondrous is the cavalcade,
All in rarest hues arrayed.
Abbâys of a thousand dyes,
Cunning-wrought embroideries:
Camels, each in gorgeous trappings
Bears its chief in costly wrappings:
Crimson housings, bridles golden,
Pendants of the ages olden.
O'er the vast primeval sand—
Poised a spear in every hand—
Many weary leagues have they
Travelled on from day to day:
Patient is the desert trod
Mid the silences of God.
Though their path has brightened been,
Sun by day and moonlight sheen,
Still the silver lamp on high,†
Symbol of some portent nigh,
Stands apart from other lights.

* Matt. ii. 1, 2. † Matt. ii. 2.

THE STORY OF JESUS.

Now it touches Gilead's heights,
Now it shows its trembling quiver
Mirrored deep in Jordan river;
Till on western shore they stand—
Safely reached the border land.
Only once the star is gone:
But they journey bravely on,
Until stooping o'er the well
Again its gleam is visible.*
Joyful hailed—the longed-for ray
Takes them where the young child lay.†
Loaded bales were there unrolled,
Offerings of worth untold,
Fragrant incense, myrrh and gold.‡
Then, adoring, they too sing—
    "GLORY TO THE NEW-BORN KING!"

. . . . .

Owning thus the Holy Saviour,
Rich and lowly seemed to vie,
Magi in their Orient splendour,
Shepherds in their poverty.
Pledge that those of every station—
Every tribe and tongue and nation—
Would accept the great salvation.§

* Tradition regarding the Well of Bethlehem.
† Matt. ii. 9, 10.   ‡ Matt. ii. 11.   § Is. lx. 6, 7

III

[*Simeon enters the Temple leaning on a pilgrim's staff. Mary and Joseph, attired in humble dress, come hither also with the child Jesus from Bethlehem. They have the rite of purification performed "according to the custom of the law"; carrying with them the offering provided for the poor of the people—a pair of turtledoves, or two young pigeons.*]—LUKE II. 25.

Though for long years compelled to wait,
Now does the aged Simeon hail
The future Hope of Israël
Within the Golden Temple-gate.

A yearning church had strained to hear
The sweet chimes of the advent bell.
At last the longed-for cadence fell
Upon the Saint's entrancëd ear.

The wish and prayer of trembling lips
Were now in God's good time fulfilled:
With holy joy his bosom thrilled
At the Divine Apocalypse!

To him the promise had been given
'His pilgrimage he would not close—
Not in the sleep of death repose,
Nor enter on the bliss of heaven,—

Until his dimming eyes had seen
Messiah promised to his race.' *
He gazed upon His Blessed face
With no obscuring veil between.

The lowly sight no questioning brings,
His simple faith all doubt disarms,
He clasps the Saviour in his arms,
And thus his "*Nunc Dimittis*" sings—

" Now let me, Lord, in peace depart,
According to Thy gracious word :
Mine eyes have seen, mine ears have heard
That thou the great Salvation art.

' Salvation '—which Thou hast prepared
For Gentile nations to embrace ;
The glory too of Israel's race.
By the Great World the gift is shared." †

Enough.—That wondrous glimpse was his.
He, bending low, his living Lord
With patriarchal grace adored.
He sought no other joy but this. ‡

Whene'er the God he serves sees meet,
He ready is to bid farewell
To all mankind.   His raptures tell
What makes both earth and Heaven complete.

The same for us !   If HE be nigh,
If we like Simeon see THE CHRIST :

* Luke ii. 26. † Luke ii. 29, 30, 31, 32.
‡ Luke ii. 28.

With that which for this Saint sufficed,
There will be nought to do *but die!*

. . . . .

"Behold! I will send my messenger, and He shall prepare the way before me: and the Lord, whom ye seek, shall suddenly come to His temple, even the Messenger of the Covenant whom ye delight in: behold! He shall come, saith the Lord of Hosts."—MAL. iii. 1.

. . . . .

[*Mary, Joseph, and the Child Jesus return to Bethlehem. Simeon for the last time leaves the Temple.*]

. . . . .

He dies! But, with the unfaltering voice of faith,
He sings once more his swan-song: and in peace
Departs: the accents thrilling on his tongue—
"MINE EYES, O LORD, HAVE THY SALVATION SEEN!"

IV

[*An Angel comes to Joseph in the night, and tells him to flee along with the Child and His mother to Egypt.*]

The lowly man of Nazareth obeys.
Evaded are the sanguinary wiles
Of the Judæan tyrant, who had sought
That infant life, which put in jeopardy
His throne and crown.* For the dread massacre
Already had the mandate issued forth.†
Rachel is soon to weep her murdered babes,
Refusing to be comforted, because
They are not ! ‡
                Onwards the three pilgrims go. §
The mediæval myth perchance was true
That cherub guardians heralded their path,
Strewing the sands with flowers, and warding off
The prowling beasts of prey. An Angel-throng
Doubtless encamped invisible around,
And shielded them from peril. Moon and stars
Would in these drear and voiceless solitudes
Turn night to day.

* Matt. ii. 13.   † Matt. ii. 16.
‡ Jer. xxxi. 15.   § Matt. ii. 14.

                         At last the weary route
Is traversed. They have reached the storied land
Wherein their fathers dwelt. Tradition says
Its earliest night was spent beneath the shade
Of sycamore which still survives.   Hard by,
A granite avenue of sphinxes led
Up to the gates of Heliopolis,
Hoary with Hebrew memories. The Nile,
Not distant, on pursued his regal way,
A thousand miles from his mysterious source,
Lined with colossal fanes and effigies
Of hideous worship : sculptured calves and bulls
[" Similitudes of ox that eateth hay "] ;
While in the distance, reared by Titan hands,
Flushed with the deepening gold of sunset, stood
The Pyramids—their tops like altar-fires
Aglow with evening sacrifice.
                                  In this
Their land of exile they remained, until
Herod had paid, with pangs of fearful death,
The penalty of his unnumbered crimes.
Then angel-guarded they return once more
Along the Plain of Sharon to their home
Amid the mountain slopes of Zebulon.

V

[*Scene: Nazareth. A Mother and Child linked hand in hand at a village well.*]

Around the Village Fountain nigh,
    Are groups of maidens led;
The water-flagons gracefully
    Are poised upon their head.

Among them One, both young and fair,
    With pensive face, is seen
To lavish her most tender care
    On Child of lowly mien.

> *It is Mary " meek and mild,"*
> *Honoured stem of Jesse's rod;*
> *Holy Mother! Holy Child!*
> *Son of Man, yet Son of God.**

Nature is beautiful around,
    Refreshed with morning showers;
The verdant mountains olive-crowned,
    The valleys lapped with flowers.

These fragrant hills He loved to climb—
The lilies plucked that decked the lea,

---

* Matt. ii. 23.

Watched from the height, the sun sublime
Sink golden in the Western sea.

. . . . .

Years of bright childhood ended now,
His hands the tools of labour plied,
That poverty and sweat of brow
Might for all time be sanctified.

With God and man in favour grown,
With every taint of self removed,
To do His Father's will alone
Was all for which He lived and loved.

Unto no youth but His was given
Freedom from sin's polluted breath:
Divine, Ideal " Flower of Heaven " !
THE CHRIST—THE CHRIST OF NAZARETH ! *

* Luke ii. 50, 51, 52.

VI

[*Assembling of the Passover Pilgrims. Journey from Nazareth to Jerusalem. Time, early Spring; the month, Nizan.*]

It draweth nigh the yearly feast,
When crowds of Pilgrims trod the way,
To keep with holy Eucharist
The Hebrew's proudest memory.*

Bedecked is spring in earliest prime
With robes of emerald. The bee
Roams over fields of fragrant thyme
And clusters of anemone.

The silver'd olive, fig and vine,
In wealth of beauty seem to vie;
All nature glows with tint divine
Beneath her azure canopy.

Across Esdraelon's battle-plain,
Along by Shechem's wooded glade,
Each village hails the festal train,
And swells the wondrous cavalcade.

* Luke ii. 41.

See how "they go from strength to strength," *
By day and night each other cheer
With voice of song, until at length
The Zion Temple-Courts appear.

In that vast host, there travelled ONE †
With holy face and heavenward eye,
Some destiny was His unknown,
They could not solve the mystery.

Ah! little did that human tide
Of life, to the great secret rise;
That He who journeyed by their side
Was the true Paschal Sacrifice!

. . . . .

The offerings made, once more the road
Is taken by the holy three;
Once more they reach their loved abode
Among the hills of Galilee.

The Youth Divine, with longing eyes,
Waits till the hour appointed brings
The summons for the Sun to rise
With healing underneath His wings. ‡

---

* Ps. lxxxiv. 7.   † Luke ii. 42   ‡ Mal. iv. 2.

THE JORDAN, NEAR THE DEAD SEA.

(To face p. 16.)

VII

[*John the Baptist. Scene: The Wilderness of Judæa and the river Jordan.*]

Hark, Hark, a trumpet-blast!
  But not with roll of martial drum,
  As if some Conqueror had come!
It was a loud and lonely voice
That bade the desert wastes rejoice;
A voice of herald-prophet, sent
To "call on all men to repent."*
No priestly robe or stole had he,
No pomp of earthly pedigree;
His mother's fingers wove with care
The mantle made of camel's hair.
His naked limbs and swarthy form
Could brave alike the heat and storm.
On Nature's altar-step he stood
And swayed the surging multitude:
The rock his pulpit, and the sky
Was overhead his canopy:
While Jordan with its rapid tide
Was hasting onward by his side,
To plunge into the tideless sea,
Its grave of awe and mystery.

* Matt. iii. 1 2.

Flock the vast crowd from far and near
The messenger of Heaven to hear.
How varied is the eager throng!
From north and west they pour along : *
From Bethel with its dreamland site,
From Achor with its frowning height:
The humble shepherd from his fold;
The lettered scribe, the warrior bold;
The proud and scornful Pharisee,
The casuistic Sadducee;
The hangers-on at Herod's court,
The sailor from the distant port;
Thither the busy trader hies,
And leaves behind his merchandise.
Strange voice! to hold with mighty spell
These gathering tribes of Israel.

. . . . . .

"Repent, Repent"—the word is given,
In name of God—in name of Heaven;
 The Kingdom of Messiah is at hand.
The axe is laid at root of tree;
And every cumberer shall be
 Cut down or burned like a fiery brand!†

. . . . . .

And louder still he raised his voice!
And bade the listening throng rejoice:
 While in majestic thunder-tone he cries,—
"Behold the branch of Jesse's rod!
Behold! behold the Lamb of God!
 The world's divine all-glorious Sacrifice!" ‡

Matt. iii. 5, 6 ; Luke iii. 14.   † Luke iii. 8, 9.
  ‡ John i. 29, 36.

Lo! as they list to what he saith,
They see the Christ of Nazareth:
Messiah promised age by age,
The world's expected heritage:
Him for whom all time had waited,
God's own Son, the Uncreated!

  . . . . .

Thus years of hope deferred had past,
And now the Advent dawns at last.
Henceforth be every idol dumb,
For Christ the Prince of Peace has come.
The Holy Jesus, Light of Light,
Stoops to receive the mystic rite:
The gracious Spirit, like a dove,
Descending from the Heavens above:
While a great voice is heard on high,
Attesting His Divinity.*

   * Luke iii. 21, 22.

VIII

[*Scene: Marriage in Cana of Galilee. Twilight. Jesus, His mother, and five disciples.**]

With waving torch and voice of song
A nuptial pageant sweeps along—
   The bridegroom and the bride:
With fruit and flowers, with wine and bread,
The village banquet-room is spread,
   At fall of eventide.

And Jesus too is there a guest:
And with His gracious presence blest
   The feast of lowly love.
He comes the festal joy to share,
And shower upon the wedded pair
   Rich blessings from above.

His mother saith "There is no wine:
Put forth, my son, Thy power divine." †
   Nor was the call delayed.
One holy word—one holy look:—
With water from the crystal brook
   The mandate is obeyed.

* John ii. 1–12. † John ii. 3.

Moses by Egypt's river stood,
And turned the water into blood ;
    But Jesus, from on high,
Transmutes the water into wine,
And sanctifies by word and sign
    Earth's fondest, holiest tie.

O happy scene ! O hallowed thought !
That He who in His mercy brought
    Salvation to our race,
Thus has the name of " Home " endeared,
Blest every family bond, and cheered
    Earth's lowliest dwelling-place !

IX

[*Scene: The Lake of Gennesaret. Its surroundings and memories.*]

Thereafter Jesus took the road
Which led "down" to the Inland Sea,*
Where future loving friends abode—
The lonely Lake of Galilee.

With dawn their journey they pursue,
Until the westering sun has set.
His slanting beams of golden hue
Still linger on Gennesaret.

In sacred thought is shrined the lake,
Along whose shores we fondly trace
His footsteps—shores he loved to make
His most abiding dwelling-place.

No lovelier spot on earth was found
Than this secluded "Temple-Shrine."
Its gardens clustering thick around
With palm and olive, fig and vine.

* John ii. 12.

The shepherd kept his watch and ward
On the green girdling hills above,
Whilst in the copsy dells was heard
The murmur of the turtle-dove.

Vast palaces on every side
Were mirrored in that sea of glass,
Amid them, towering in its pride,
The golden house of Antipas.

Oft on these mountain heights around
The early light of morn He saw,
From northern Hermon, snowy-crowned,
To purple-tinted Gadara : *

" The city set upon a hill ;" †
Whose summit was with beacon fired
When the new moon rose clear and still
And day's last glimmering light expired.

The sick, the maimed, the halt, the blind,
In grateful cool of eventide, ‡
Sought the great Saviour of mankind.
His healing touch was ne'er denied.

They crowded to the silent beach,
They met him on the lonely " Tel,"
They hung with rapture on His speech,
Both gracious word and parable. §

* Mark v. 1.   † Matt. v. 14.   ‡ Mark i. 32.
§ Matt. xiii.

Each verdant vale, each thorny brake,
Each flower, each lily of the field,*
Seem to recall the thoughts He spake—
The thronging multitudes He healed:

The mountain altars where He prayed,
The green cathedral aisles He trod,
Where, before day, He kneeling paid
Meet homage to His Father-God!

Still do His loving words sublime
Sound fresh beneath these azure skies;
The limpid waters seem to chime
With never-dying memories.

O sacred haunt!—THE HOME OF CHRIST!
To think that, on its silent shore,
He kept so long a holy "tryst,"
And hallowed it for evermore!

．　　　．　　　．　　　．　　　．　　　．

Soon ended His first visit there,
New calls of duty fall to Him,
For the next Feast He must prepare
Approaching in Jerusalem.†

* Matt. vi. 28.　　　　† John ii. 13.

X

[*Jesus goes up to the Feast of the Passover. Assemblage of the Worshippers. Caravan proceeds by the Eastern route. Valley of the Jordan. Jerusalem is approached by the Jericho road and Mount of Olives.*]

It has come! the Festal Season,
And the eager crowds are mustering
By the cities of the Lake-side:
Proselytes of every nation;
Pilgrims from the northern regions;
Israelites from far Damascus;
From the shores of Tyre and Sidon,
From the Tigris and Euphrates,
Wearing striped abbây and caftan.
Armed are some with martial weapons.
Leading camels bearing spices,
Gilead balm and fragrant incense;—
Costly bales of festal raiment:
Broideries of cunning workers:
Coops of doves of varied plumage
Cooing in their wicker cages,
Brought from valleys of Orontes
Or the wooded glades of Hermon,
To supply the Temple offerings.

Soon the caravan is moving
Slow along the western highway.
Soon they leave the inland waters
With their busy life behind them;
Entering the gorge of Jordan
With the beetling cliffs of limestone
Fringed with terebinth and ilex;
While the tribute streams are rushing
(Which the latter rains have flooded)
Swift to swell the "Great Descender:"*
Each its louder mountain music
Mingling with the lofty pæans
Chanted by the minstrel pilgrims.
All the journey is historic,
Every memory inspiring—
Here the ancient home of Jephthah;
Here was nursed the great Elijah
Mid the savage glens of Gilead.
Here the scenes of David's exile,
Where he sang the dirge of dirges
O'er the child of his affections.
Here the veteran Barzillai
Travelled from his mountain-dwelling
That he might do loyal homage
With his band of bold retainers
To the Victor King of Judah.
 Soon the Dead Sea's sullen waters
Gleamed beneath its burning ridges;
While the purple range of Moab
Like a bastion built by giants
Brightly shone in fires of sunset.

   * Name of the Jordan.

Or they travelled in the starlight,
Through the gloomy vale of Achor,
Echoing to the festal music.
Upwards, onwards, still they hasten,
Mid the buzz of pilgrim voices,
And through fields of vernal beauty
Till they hail the " mid-way fountain"
And have reached the Mount of Olives.
Then, across the Vale of Kedron,
Gaze they on the towers of Zion,
And the Temple in its splendour,
Throned amid the girdling mountains :
God's own city—Queen of ages,
He her Refuge and Defender.

. . . . .

ONE amid the festal throng
Comes with voice of holy song
To rehearse the Paschal story,
Jesus Christ—THE KING OF GLORY!

XI

[*The Temple is cleansed of its traffickers. Scene: Nicodemus, a Jewish Ruler, alone in his house in Jerusalem. He resolves to have an interview with Jesus. A Soliloquy.*]

Yes, I shall go to Him by night,
And steal amid the olive glades,
When day withdraws its garish light
And the last glow of sunset fades.

May I not tell Him all I feel?
This Heavenly Teacher sent from God,*
In hushed seclusion may reveal
What dare not be proclaimed abroad.

The longings of a yearning heart
His wisdom and His love may meet;
New views of truth He may impart,
While sitting docile at His feet.

. . . . . .

'Tis done: the Ruler tremblingly
Sets forth to keep the holy tryst,
The moon and silent stars on high
Conduct him to the home of Christ. †

* John iii. 2. † *Ibid.*

That Home, perchance a leafy bower,
Its floor with falling dewdrops wet ;
Yet hallowed evermore the hour
Together spent on Olivet.

O glorious message for all time !
O glorious words that cannot die !
" *For God* so *loved the world !* "—their chime
Goes echoing through eternity ! *

. . . . . .

That interview at dead of night
Did Nicodemus ne'er forget.
Though lost for two long years from sight,
His heart was ready when they met

To manifest its gratitude ;
For when was slain the Christ adored,
In Pilate's house he boldly stood
And begged the body of his Lord. †

So great the gain compared with loss,
So great his love for Him who died ;
He thinks not of the shameful cross—
He glories in the Crucified !

* John iii. 16.   † John xix. 39.

XII

[*Scene: El-Mûkna. Jacob's Well. Noontide. A woman approaches with a pitcher of water.*]

  Nigh the old town of Shechem
   El-Mûkna's plain is seen;
  But it is decked no longer
   In robes of summer green.*

  Fit for the harvest sickles
   It waves with golden grain,
  And soon the songful reapers
   Will bind their sheaves again. †

  A little band of Pilgrims
   Recline with weary feet,
  Beside the well of Jacob,
   Faint with the noontide heat. ‡

  The weariest ONE is seated
   Upon the Fountain's rim:
  While soaring in the distance
   Is hoary Gerizim. §

* John iv. 35.   † John iv. 35.   ‡ John iv 6, 8.
        § John iv. 20.

A woman of Samaria
    Its water comes to share;
She little knows the Traveller,
    Who rapt in thought is there.*

He tells her of a Fountain
    Whose water never fails,†
A living stream perennial
    A bliss that never pales.

She listens to the story
    The Pilgrim Jew has told:
The mists her soul which shrouded
    Are from that hour unrolled.

Found is the great Messiah; ‡
    She sees Him face to face,
And, strong in faith, becometh
    A trophy of His grace!

The pardoning love of Jesus,
    So amply here bestowed,
Enshrines in holiest memory
    This gospel Episode.

* John iv. 6, 7.   † John iv. 10.   ‡ John iv. 29.

XIII

[*After a brief visit to the Lake, Jesus returns to Jerusalem for the Feast of Purim. Scene: The Pool of Bethesda.*] *

[*Imaginary words of the Cripple seated on the outer rim of the pool, whither he had resorted for thirty-eight years, waiting for the Angel to come down from Heaven to trouble the water.*]

Long I've lain by this Bethesda,
Left in anguish to endure:
Come, great Angel! stir the waters:
   Give me cure. †

Years on years I've failed to mingle
With the joyous festive throng,
Hearing only in the distance
   Paschal song.

---

* I may here say that, amid the perplexities of Harmonists, I have followed the sequence of events in the sacred narrative adopted.
   † John v. 2–5.

Sad the blare of silver trumpets:
For to me they sound in vain;
Here in lone unsuccoured silence
    I remain.

Oft in waiting for the summons
Nimbler feet have distanced mine.
O with strong hand come to help me
    Power divine!*

[*Jesus of Nazareth is seen approaching, and thus speaks—*]

Tell me, child of suffering, wilt thou
Be made whole? Then take thy bed,
Rise! and be thy heart, long broken,
    Comforted. †

. . . . .

Then he rose, no more a cripple
Weak and weary, lone and sad;
That one gracious word of healing
    Makes him glad. ‡

Nature her sealed book re-opens;
Sights and sounds to him unknown,
Long alone enjoyed by others,
    Now his own!

* John v. 7.   † John v 6-8.
   ‡ John v. 9.

Therewith ends his "night of weeping,"
And afresh with sandals shod
Forth he hastens, "walking, leaping,
      Praising God."

In the Temple-Courts we find him,*
Seeking grateful to record
Vows that shall for ever bind him
      To the Lord.

* John v. 14.

XIV

[*Jesus leaves in the middle of the Feast, and goes to Nazareth, where he is rejected. He pays a long and memorable visit to the Lake of Gennesaret. Season, Spring.*]

Then the Lord renews His journey
    Northward toward the inland sea;
Passing through His native village
    In the hills of Galilee.

Vernal sunshine floods the landscape,
    Verdure decks the woodlands fair,
From the almond, fig, and olive,
    To the modest maidenhair.

Every varied tint and colour
    In the race of beauty vies,
As if angels had been weaving
    Heavenly embroideries.

Cliffs of limestone rise above Him,
    Corn-clad valleys smile beneath,
Till He stands beneath the threshold
    Of His native Nazareth.*

* Luke iv. 16.

In the Synagogue, while paying
   His devotions as of old,
Standing up He reads the saying
   By the Prophet thus foretold :—*

"*The Spirit of the Lord upon me*
   Hath anointed me to sound
Good tidings to the meek and lowly,
   Liberty to captives bound:

"*Comfort to all the broken-hearted,*
   Setting those in prison free;
To earth's remotest regions bearing
   Trumpet tones of Jubilee."

† "Sitting down" He said, "This Scripture
   Is to you fulfilled to-day.
I AM HE—the World's Redeemer—
   Who has come its debt to pay."

     .   .   .   .

But they will not hear the message,
   Rudely they reject His claim :
Seeking loudly with their curses
   To impeach His spotless name. ‡

To a pinnacle they lead Him,
   Jutting high above the town,
Threat'ning from its rocky ridges
   Headlong thence to cast Him down. §

---

* Isa. lxi. 1, 2 ; Luke iv. 16–19.   † Luke iv. 20, 21.
‡ Luke iv. 28, 29.   § Luke iv. 29.

Primal taste the Man of Sorrows
    Has of griefs profounder still!
Then with saddened heart and lonely
    Crosses He the eastern hill;

Till He finds Himself in safety,
    Far beyond the scorner's reach,
Listening to the gentle wavelets
    Rippling on the pebbly beach.*

* Luke iv. 30, 31.

XV

[*Scene: The Lake of Gennesaret. Season, late in Autumn. Jesus teaches the people out of a boat close to the shore.*]

    The year has waned; the nights are long;
    Hushed is the gush of summer song;
        The heat has disappeared.
    The Lake is swept with cooling breeze,
    Bared are the woods: or else the trees
        With autumn tints are seared.

    Early we see a motley crowd;
    With hum of voices waxing loud,
        They line the circling bay.
    A boat in which a stranger stands,
    Whose stern has cleared the shelving sands,
        Rocks in the wavelets' play.*

    They gather round with bated breath
    To hear the Christ of Nazareth!
        They watch His face serene:

* Luke v. 1—3.

Speak of His miracle divine,
The turning water into wine
    At Cana's marriage scene.

The first is this of many an hour
He preached in tones of wondrous power
    To thronging hearers met :
And consecrated for all time
Alike with works and words sublime
    Thy shores GENNESARET!

"*And the common people heard Him gladly.*" *

* Mark xii. 37.

XVI

[*Scene: Gennesaret. An imagined calm on the Lake. The Apostles are called and consecrated by Jesus. Time, early noon.*]

The crowd disperses: and alone remain
The fishermen, who through the livelong night
Have toiled unrecompensed. Close to the shore,
Two are employed extracting from their nets *
The cumbering rack and weed: while other two
Are mending them. † Let fancy paint the scene!
Nature is cradled in voluptuous sleep;
And flooded is the beautiful expanse
With molten gold—a hush of halcyon calm.
The sea and sky seem wed in peaceful love.
No tremulous ripples breaking on the beach
Disturb the fragile craft. These villagers,
Weary and jaded with their vigils long,
With hope anticipate successful gains
After the sun has set: when crescent moon
And stars come forth in the blue heaven above
To cheer them. Simon listens to a voice
Whose music oft in future he will hear.
It is his Lord! commanding him to make

* Luke v. 5.   † Luke v. 3.

A circuit round the cove.* At once with oar
The summons is obeyed. He launches forth
Amid the quiet waters, mirroring
Now rock and thorny nâbk, now plumaged fern
Or tapering reed. In simple faith he says—
"Nevertheless, Lord, at Thy Word supreme,
I shall let down the net."† Immediately
Its meshes with the unexpected spoil
Are strained to breaking. Multitudes of fish
Reward obedience: for the vessels sink
With the astounding capture.‡ Peter falls
Adoring at the feet of Jesus! Then,
With trembling lip, low kneeling, he exclaims—
"Depart from me, a sinful man, O Lord!"§
The Lord addresses him. "Fear not," saith He,
"From henceforth thou shalt sink a nobler net
Enclosing in its drag immortal souls!"‖
Thus the mute tenants of that inland sea
Were made a pledge and parable, for all
Who, faithful to their calling, would reclaim
The perishing, the outcast, and the lost,
From ocean-depths of sin to deathless life!

．　　．　　．　　．　　．　　．　　．

The brothers, forthwith, bring their boats to land.
From that time, onward, willingly they leave
Their earthly all to follow in His steps: ¶
The hallowed scenes of youth relinquishing,
The sheltered bays and nooks they loved so well;
Bright home of their affections; pensive hours

* Luke v. 4. † Luke v. 5. ‡ Luke v. 7.
§ Luke v. 8. ‖ Luke v. 10. ¶ Luke v. 11.

Out in the midnight sea: the silent stars
Shedding their silvery lustre. Following, too,
No leader laurel-crowned,—with soul inspired
By "winged ambitions," but of lowly birth:
The homeless Christ of Galilee; who oft
Had not the couch whereon to lay His Head,
Save on the dewy grass;—His lullaby
The night wind, or the neighbouring brook, which
    sang
Its tuneful way along the olive dells.
Counting the cost, the price was gladly paid.
From the resolve of that momentous day
They swerved not. Loyal to their Master's call,
Their boats and homes and friends at once were left.
They had the best—the choicest recompense,
Possession now of blessings manifold,
And in the world to come—Eternal Life! *

.   .   .   .   .   .

O Blessed Christ of Nazareth! while here,
In this pathetic scene of holy times,
Earth's common drudgery transfigured is
By Thy commanding word and made divine:
Thou hast a consecration greater still for those
Who give ungrudging effort to enclose
Thousands within the gospel-net: and cast
Trophies of grace unnumbered at Thy feet;
The gathered spoils of Heaven for Evermore!

* Luke xviii. 30.

XVII

[*Jesus continues all night in devotion. In the morning He joins the disciples and the multitude, and preaches the Sermon on the Mount.*]

    A rocky hill His " Altar stair,"
    His kneeling place the dewy sod :
    He spending hours of night in prayer—
        Beneath the stars of God ! *

    A solemn silence reigns around,
    The oracles of nature dumb,
    Hushed the continuous traffic sound
        Within Capernaum.

    Nought is there heard upon the Lake,
    Save now and then the dash of oar,
    Or as the tiny wavelets break
        Their ripples on the shore.

    At last the flush of morning steals,†
    The midnight shadows cease to fall,
    And regal Hermon first reveals
        His golden coronal.

    * Luke vi. 12.   † Luke vi. 13.

The Lord of Life and Light descends.
Mid opening flowers and pearly clouds
To a green slope His pathway wends:—
    He meets the multitudes.*

.   .   .   .   .

What does He teach that varied crowd?
Is it in praise of deeds of old?
Are warrior trumpets blaring loud
    And carnage red extolled?

Is it that intellect alone,
Upsoaring with its eagle eye,
Can gather trophies else unknown,
    With proud philosophy?

Is it the baser lust of power?
The mighty trampling on the weak,
That riches are the only dower
    For human hearts to seek?

Nay rather "blessed" who rejoice
To stem the rage of evil's flood:—
"The battle with confusëd noise
    And garments rolled in blood."

Not haughty Pharisees and Scribes
On rites, and forms, and fasts who dwell:
But lowly hearts compose the tribes
    Of His believing Israel.

        * Luke vi. 17.

Blest above all is every mind
Who feels it "noble to be good,"
The pure, the merciful, the kind,
    Earth's holiest brotherhood.

To a whole world with anguish torn,
Distracted with ten thousand feuds,
He uttered on that early morn
    His great beatitudes :—

Blessed are the poor in spirit: for theirs is the Kingdom of Heaven.

Blessed are they that mourn: for they shall be comforted.

Blessed are the meek: for they shall inherit the Earth.

Blessed are they that hunger and thirst after righteousness: for they shall be filled.

Blessed are the merciful: for they shall obtain mercy.

Blessed are the pure in heart: for they shall see God.

Blessed are the peacemakers: for they shall be called the children of God.*

"He taught them as one having authority, and not as the Scribes."†

* Matt. v. 3-10.   † Matt. vii. 29.

XVIII

[*Jesus comes down from the Mount of Beatitudes, and, crossing the plain of Gennesaret, enters the city of Capernaum: where He heals the Centurion's servant.*]

One who had deeds of valour done,
Herodian soldier bold and brave—
Comes pleading for his dying slave—
It is the " good Centurion." *

Perhaps though with a warrior's pride
On Campus Martius oft he stood,
Though in his veins runs Roman blood,
All boastful thought he lays aside ;—

Forgets the memories that stir
The hero heart. With eager breath
He seeks the Christ of Nazareth,
The great yet lowly Comforter.†

Wrung with true grief his heart has been—
His servant is about to die :
The King of Terrors passes by :
No human help can intervene !

* Matt. viii. 5, 6. † Luke v. 15.

Remembering that close of day,
When crowds around the feet of Christ
Had gathered ;—and a look sufficed
To bid disease and death away :—

The faithful suppliant felt assured,
By the same word of prompt command,
By which he ruled his legion-band,
The prostrate servant would be cured.*

And so it was; the parting breath
Is soon recalled. The sufferer weak
Has health remounting on his cheek—
The Lord of Life has conquered death.†

The valiant soldier, looking back
When duty called to face the foe,
Or sitting by the watch-fire's glow
Beside the nightly bivouac ;—

Would doubtless lovingly recall
The Lord's ability to save ;
The rescue from the early grave,—
The love that had transcended all.

And when war-trumpets cease to blare,
When martial triumphs shall decay,
And victor laurels fade away,
Live shall this deed of faith and prayer.‡

---

* Matt. viii. 8, 9.   † Matt. viii. 13.   ‡ Matt. viii. 10.

XIX

[*Scene: Jesus and His disciples, after leaving the Lake of Galilee, are seen walking along the road, on the slope of Little Hermon, to Nain. Time, Sunset.*]

They have early crossed Mount Tabor,
   With its rounded summit high;
Reached the borders of Esdrælon
   Israel's golden granary.

There the hamlet-town of Nain
   On its rocky ridges smiled,
Linked for ever with the story
   Of the widow and her child.*

[*The disciples address their Lord.*]

"Master, see that crowd approaching!"
   Then was heard a muffled wail,
Like the pulsing throb of dirges
   Borne upon the evening gale.

One was slowly seen advancing
   Toward the place of burial nigh,
Tears, and sackcloth rent, are telling
   Of a mother's agony.†

* Luke vii. 11.   † Luke vii. 12.

NAIN.

(To face p. 48.)

[*Christ has compassion on her: speaks to her: and brings her dead son to life.*]

Weep not! Trust the Lord who giveth
    Comfort to all those who mourn:
Dry thy tears; thy dead one liveth,
    Thou, no more, shalt be forlorn!*

Sudden is the bier forsaken;
    Sudden hushed each plaintive sound;
"This my son—again he liveth!
    He was lost, but now is found!" †

"Lost and found!" the joyous refrain,
    Lost and found!—She grateful cries:
"Take the heart, Lord, Thou hast gladdened,
    As a life-long sacrifice!"
  .   .   .   .   .   .

Gaze with wonder the disciples
    On the youth so lately dead,
While they whisper to each other,
    "It was God Himself who said,—

'Leave thy helpless orphaned children,
    They preserved shall ever be ·
Let thy sorely stricken widows
    Trust their broken hearts to Me.'" ‡

* Luke vii. 13.   † Luke vii. 15.   ‡ Jer. xlix. 11.

XX

[Jesus meets the woman who was a sinner, at a feast in the house of Simon the Pharisee. City of Capernaum.]

No gladder note of music steals
Upon the ears of wanderers lost,
Than when *Himself* the Lord reveals
"A Saviour to the uttermost."

A guilty child of sin and shame,
With "outcast" branded on her brow,[*]
A trophy of His grace became
And made the penitential vow—

Of love and loyalty to Him
Who changed her bondage to release,
Who dried her eyes, with weeping dim,
And spake the longed-for word of peace.

A bird was she, with broken wing
And struggling efforts to be free,
Striving in vain lost notes to sing
That cheered her guileless infancy;

Confronted by a blighted past,
The memories of a ruined home:

[*] Luke vii. 36, 37.

An ever-gloomy sky o'ercast
The wilds so long she loved to roam.

O to get back life's joyous morn,
The sunshine of her early day!
To weave afresh the robe so torn,
And save its threads from more decay.

Thus seeking rest and finding none,
She hears of Him who rest can give,
Who can redeem the years undone,
And cause the dead in sin to live!

She longs to reach that Saviour's feet,
Lay there the burden of her fears.
To see His face she is not meet:
May she make mute appeal with tears?

Unbidden to the feast she goes.
In trembling awe she cowers behind
Her Lord.   She tells her tale of woes
With quivering lip.   Her hands unbind

The tresses falling from her head,—
The ripples of dishevelled hair,
And wipes with them His feet.   He read*
And answered her unuttered prayer!

The cynic guests around that board
May brand with cruel taunts her shame,†
But One is there, beloved, adored,
Who has a higher, nobler aim—

---

* Luke vii. 38.   † Luke vii. 39.

To raise the trodden, prostrate flower,
Uplift its tendrils from the dust,
And turn that penitential hour
To one of faith, and love, and trust.

'Tis done!—Her fettered soul is free,
Allayed and hushed her brooding fears;
Forth goes to light and liberty,
This gospel "Niobe all tears!" *

In her is solved the anxious quest—
" Is there for me such grace divine?
Can Christ to weary ones give rest?
Can He forgive such guilt as mine?

" Say, will He hear my prayerful cry,
My base, defiling touch endure?
O dare I ever venture nigh
To One so infinitely pure?"

Yes, the most hopeless, ruined, lost,
May at the gates of mercy knock;
The bark, mid wildest waters tossed,
Be moored to the Eternal Rock!

She breaks her box of precious nard,
The only tribute she can give
Of gratitude to Him who heard
Her prayer, and made it worth to live.†

The balm-word for her tale of woe,
Light amid darkness deep and dense,
Are pledges from the long ago
Of peace for trembling penitence! ‡

---

* Luke vii. 47, 48.   † Luke vii. 38.   ‡ Luke vii. 47-50.

XXI

[*The daughter of Jairus. Jairus alone in the room of his dying child at his house at Capernaum.*]

[*Jairus. A soliloquy.*]

My daughter, little daughter,* dearly prized,
Thou art about to die! The sands are running
Fast to their final grain. I love to think
Of all thou art, of all which thou hast been
In cherished years irrevocably gone!
Oft have we wandered, clasping hand in hand,
Beneath the shade of silver olive-boughs,
Picking the wild-flowers from the copsy dells,
Or tiny treasures from the shell-strewn shore;
Skimming with snow-white sail that summer sea,
Watching the play of light and shadow on
The hills of Gadara : and, best of all,
The summer of an ever-radiant soul.
Affection never was so fully bound
To my own child, as now. My future is
Close interwoven day by day with thee—
The promised solace of my waning years.
Sad, sad indeed, that she whose gentle hand

* Mark v. 23.

Erased the wrinkles from this brow, and oft
With offices of filial love had sped,—
A ministering Angel ; who, methought,
My dying pillow would be spared to smooth ;
Is soon to moulder in the dust of death !
Are life's best hopes and visions to become
Only a memory, and I left to wail
The plaintive dirge of Israel's weeping seer—
" How broken is my staff and beauteous rod ?"*
The King of Terrors nearing stealthily
To rob me of my one surviving joy :
Each moment hastening the crisis-hour
When all that binds me to this heart of hearts
Is torn asunder ! My horizon once
Was bright with golden clouds. Draped are they now
In doleful sackcloth. O, can nothing storm
Death's iron citadel ! and this tender prey
Compel him to relinquish ? *Twelve years old !*
Just when the budding leaves are pearled with dew
Of early morning, and the sun of life
Has, long ere reaching its meridian, set.
The music of that voice for ever hushed !
The treasure taken when most dearly prized,
And when most needed ! Dread, remorseless foe !
Have pity on me, and recall once more
My fading lily to its loveliness !
Spare it to shed fresh fragrance on my path
And make my home again a paradise.

· · · · · ·

* Jer. xlviii. 17.

[*Jairus continues*—]

One, One alone there is, who can avail
In this o'erwhelming sorrow. I will haste
To the Great Teacher—Christ of Nazareth;
He who restored the Roman slave: I know
His might combined with kindness. I shall rush
To His dear feet and ask imploringly
To save my child!* With His reviving touch
The ebbing tides may come to flow again.
Sowing in tears I yet may reap in joy;
God of my Fathers—Answerer of prayer!
Hear the mute voice of these my pleading tears,
And give me back my daughter!

. . . . . .

[*Jesus stands by the bedside.*]

She is not dead but sleepeth.† "Fear ye not,
Only believe!" ‡ Ye hirĕd minstrels, hush
Your simulated dirges. Mock no more
The majesty of death with mimic sounds.
Quickly depart ye! §

. . . . . .

Then the Lord of Life,
Bending in anguish o'er the silent couch,
The summons gives! Forth does the mandate
    go—
"*I say to thee arise!*" ‖ The sleeper wakes.

* Luke viii. 41; Mark v. 23.
† Luke viii. 52. ‡ Mark v 36
§ Matt. ix. 23, 24; Mark v. 38-40.
‖ Mark v. 41.

Raises the prostrate flower its drooping head.
Tears of deep anguish turn to songs of joy,
And Death with outspread wings has fled away.

Thus Jesus did restore the loved and lost:
Set, once again, the bow within the cloud,
And wrote in lettering of gleaming gold—
JEHOVAH ROPHI! God hath healëd thee.*

* Ex. xv. 26.

XXII

[*Death of John the Baptist. The sorrow of the disciples and their Master. Gathering of the multitude on the north-east of the Lake, and the miracle of the Loaves which followed.*]

Nigh to the Dead Sea's gloomy shores
There stood Machærus' fortress walls;
A foul and fatal deed has stained
   Its festive halls.

The dismal tidings just have come
Of the Great Baptist's cruel death;
The sorrowing twelve are stricken dumb.*
   Their Master saith—

"Our best-belovëd friend is gone,
Let us our saddened hearts beguile
In some secluded desert place,
   And rest awhile." †

A glorious human sun has set:
Undimmed the radiance to its close.
Faithful and true—his holy life
   No shadow throws.

  * Matt. xiv. 10–12.   † Mark vi. 31.

If dirgeful waves refuse to sleep,
Chiming a love that cannot die,
They will the tryst of sorrow keep
    Where none is nigh.

Away from noisy crowds—the hush
Of some deep solitude "apart,"
Whose loneliness may help to sooth
    The smitten heart.*

Their fishing craft makes for the strand
Where Jordan in its ample tide
Flows through dense reeds, while cattle browse
    On every side.†

Befitting seems the chosen place
For musings in that sacred hour,
Mourning a soul replete throughout
    With hero-power;

To quit the world's ungenial throng,
The "loud and stunning tide" of life,
And hush amid lone Nature's calm
    Earth's jarring strife.

To none more grateful than to Him,
The glorious central Orb of Light,
Thus prematurely called to mourn
    His satellite.

. . . . . .

But brief their season of repose.
Their bark, retarded by the wind,
Has failed to reach the destined port;
    And now they find

---

* Mark vi. 32.   † Mark vi. 32.

That crowds from all the cities round
Are waiting when they shipped their oars.
Both old and young with eager steps,
        Have thronged the shores.

Some have pursued the camel-track,
Some sped across the fringe of sand ;
Vine-dressers, shepherds, villagers,
        Have swelled the band.*

The Lord beholds the multitude
Wide scattered on the gentle steep ;
They seem a flock unshepherded
        Of wandering sheep. †

Soon are His words of comfort borne
To yearning souls oppressed and sad :
"The wilderness and desert place
        He maketh glad."

The Passover was drawing nigh.
Doubtless of themes He taught the crowd
The chief of all was of Himself—
        True Lamb of God!

. . . .

But now it is the evening hour.
The near surrounding mountains fling
Their shadows on the plain. The sun
        Is westering.

How shall these hungering throngs be fed,
Thus gathered in that lonely waste ?
The scanty contents of their scrip
        They scarce can taste.

---

* Matt. xiv. 13.   † Mark vi. 34.

No stores for sale of loaves or fruit:
No booth or hostelry is nigh;
No money in the common purse
        With which to buy.

A morsel from some barley loaves
And two small fishes of the lake;
How few among their number can
        Of these partake! *

The grassy hillocks all around
Are verdant with the rains of spring,
One floral carpet: † while the birds
        In copses sing.

Raising His loving eyes to Heaven
He doled the portions where He stood;
With the disciples' aid He fed
        The multitude.

"Cause them to sit in rows," He said;
And thus, surrounding Nature's board,
The loaves and fishes were dispensed
        By the good Lord.

Although five thousand mouths were filled,
Twelve baskets full remained to tell
The Christ of Nazareth had wrought
        A miracle. ‡

They would have longed to hail Him King,
And deck His brow with regal crown;
But He no aspirations had
        For such renown

---

* Mark vi. 37, 38.   † Mark vi. 39.   ‡ Mark vi. 37-44.

At last the festal crowds retire :
Singing with joy their Paschal hymn—
"Our feet shall stand within thy gates,
          Jerusalem !"

Again the little ship is manned,
The faithful twelve the anchor weigh :
Their Master to a neighbouring hill,
          Retires to pray.

XXIII

[*Night on the Lake of Gennesaret. The fishermen-disciples are overtaken with a tempest. Their Lord comes to them walking on the Sea.*]

A hollow moaning sound
Sweeps down the hills around,
   The premonition of a coming storm.*
In the approaching dark
He tells them to embark.
   What He commands they faithfully perform.

Toiling with baffled oar
To reach the distant shore,
   They try their mutual terrors to assuage.
But mid the surging swell,
With cries inaudible,
   In vain they try to hush the tempest's rage.†

[*The disciples, alone on the water, say to one another—*]

"Where is the Master gone?
Why leave us here alone,
   Amid the trough of this tempestuous sea?

* Matt. xiv. 22.   † Matt. xiv. 24.

No gleam in midnight sky—
The billows surging high,
   Our Master! O, our Master! Where is He?

"If only He were here,
Our faithless hearts to cheer,
   These seething waters would upheave in vain.
But now our foundering bark
Is powerless, in the dark,
   To wrestle with the blinding hurricane!"

   .   .   .   .   .

Far on a mountain height,
Which clouds have veiled from sight,
   The Christ again His oratory rears.
With God He intercedes,
For His disciples pleads,
   With His strong prayers He would dispel their fears.*

Climbing these "Altar-stairs,"
Mid wolf and jackal lairs,
   Beneath the moon and stars' still silent reign,
The Lord of Earth and Heaven
Beholds the tempest-driven,
   Their plaintive pleadings do not rise in vain.

Lo, on the crested wave
He draweth nigh to save!
   Loudly, above the moaning of the blast,
The calming word is said—
"'Tis I, be not afraid"—
   It is the longed-for Saviour come at last.†

   * Luke xiv. 23.   † Luke xiv. 25, 26.

At first, in trembling awe,
It seems as if they saw
   Some phantom-spirit from the deep abyss.
Soon at that mighty Voice
They, reassured, rejoice:
   They feel forthwith no longer comfortless.*

    .   .   .   .   .   .

How oft when hid from sight,
In "fourth watch of the night" †
   The Heavenly Pilot nears our spirits tossed.
He speaks the soothing word!
The anguished cry is heard:
   He proves "a Saviour to the uttermost."

We saw His radiant form,
In midst of wave and storm,
   Shine through the mystery of darkness dim.
He answered has our prayer;
" We went through flood, ... and THERE,"
   (In sorrow's pathway) "we rejoiced in Him!" ‡

* Luke xiv. 26, 27.   † Luke xiv. 25.   ‡ Ps. lxvi. 6.

PLAIN OF GENNESARET.

(To face p. 64.)

XXIV

[*Jesus leaves the Lake of Gennesaret for Cæsarea-Philippi. Its choice situation and surroundings. The confession of the Apostles regarding the divine claims of Christ. His address to St. Peter. The impregnable Rock. The announcement of His sufferings and death.*]

 His earthly sun is soon to set!
  For the last time, before He dies,
  He gathers farewell memories
 Of his own loved Gennesaret.

 The road which skirted Merom's Lake,
  And other spots of old renown,
  Led to where Philip built a town,
 And for his royal master's sake,

 Linked Cæsar's name along with his.*
  A famed resort in summer-time,
  When verdure clad its rock sublime—
 A northern Acropolis.

 Fled many from the sultry plain
  To where the upland breezes blow;
  And from its throne of virgin snow
 Great Hermon seemed a king to reign.†

* Cæsarea-Philippi, Matt. xvi. 13.
† Modern name, Jebel-es-Sheikh (The Kingly Mountain).

Here in Greek legend Panias dwells;*
  The Jordan, in impetuous might,
  Bursts from its cave: while on the height
A temple rears its pinnacles.

What prospects thence! The mid-day sun
  Like golden lamp lit all the land.
  Far off, Beersheba's stretch of sand,
And near, the heights of Lebanon.

Nature did lavishly provide
  Fresh features: from the arrowy rush
  Of Jordan, to the pensive hush
Of crimson-tinted eventide.

Beneath that charm of land and sky,
  Christ, to the twelve with anxious fear
  Lest the great mission might appear
A failure,—with a burdened sigh,

Questions their inmost thoughts of Him.
  Were their fond hopes unrealised?
  Doomed to extinction all they prized?
Their former bright horizon dim?

Then Simon speaks for all the rest,
  In name of the disciple-band,
  Responsive to his Lord's demand—
"Thou art the Son of God confessed." †

---

* The heathen god *Pan* corrupted into the modern *Panias*.
† Matt. xvi. 16.

Enough.   The answer that was given
　　Restored His gladness.   Scarce a trace
　　Of sorrow left : once more His face
Seemed to reflect the light of Heaven.

"That rock," said He, "and Temple high
　　In fragments may bestrew the ground;
　　Not so the Kingdom which I found,
Its lifetime is Eternity.

"No word of Mine shall ever fail;
　　Left is no promise unfulfilled.
　　Against the living church I build
The gates of Hell shall not prevail." *

　　.　　.　　.　　.　　.

[*Some days subsequently.*]

As ofttimes Nature's brightest sky
　　Is sombred o'er with weeping clouds :
　　So now, unlooked-for darkness shrouds.
He tells the twelve that He must die !†

Sad beyond words the news to them
　　Of pang and suffering soon to come;
　　Trembling with fears, and stricken dumb,
Their thoughts are toward Jerusalem !

Only the closer seemed to bind
　　Their love to Him the Son of Man.
　　He leaves the shrine of heathen Pan
And hastens on to save mankind !

* Matt. xvi. 18.　　† Matt. xvi. 21.

XXV

[*The Transfiguration-scene. Night: Mount Hermon, near Cæsarea-Philippi. Christ, with Peter, James, and John.*]

    The moonlight shone all glorious
        Above on Hermon's Hill,*
    The silence was unbroken
        By stream or murmuring rill.

    In company of Jesus
        We watch the favoured three,
    Their hearts are conscious throbbing
        With some great mystery.†

    As the deep awe of midnight
        Invests the lonely place,
    Slowly a brilliant halo
        Surrounds the Master's face.‡

    His figure is apparelled
        In robes of glistering white,
    Like to the snow in lustre
        Which lingered on the height.§

* Matt. xvii. 1.   ‡ Matt. xvii. 2; Luke ix. 29.
† Luke ix. 28.   § Mark ix. 3; Luke ix. 29.

DISTANT VIEW OF MOUNT HERMON.

(To face p. 63.)

While Moses and Elias,*
  Two noble saints above,
Have left their thrones of glory—
  Their Heaven of light and love—

That they may bear twin witness
  To their great Lord's "decease," †
The struggle hour of mortal power
  Which waits the Prince of Peace.

Then Simon Peter ardent cries,
  In mingled joy and fear,
"Let us erect three sanctuaries;
  'Tis good, Lord, to be here." ‡

But Jesus heeds him not—the scene
  Is only meant to strengthen faith,
To brace disciples faltering,
  And nerve their loving Lord for death.

The holy Christ descends the hill, §
  The stars have ceased the sky to gem;
And stedfastly He sets His face
  To go up to Jerusalem.‖

"I HAVE A BAPTISM TO BE BAPTISED WITH: AND HOW AM I STRAITENED TILL IT BE ACCOMPLISHED?"—Luke xii. 50.

* Mark ix. 4, 5.   † Luke ix. 31.   ‡ Luke ix. 33.
§ Luke ix. 37.   ‖ Luke ix. 57.

XXVI

[Scene: Jerusalem. The Feast of Tabernacles. Jesus declares Himself to be the Light of the World. On the eighth day water is brought from the Pool of Siloam. Jesus unfolds Himself as the " Giver of Living Water."]

Finished was the Jewish Harvest,
    Autumn fruits were gathered in,
Grapes were plucked from terraced vineyards,
    Oil of olive stored within

The ample jars; while festal Pilgrims
    To the Holy City wend:
Every distant home and hamlet
    Does its living tribute send.

Boughs of green and shady branches
    In festoons and arches meet;
Leafy tents and flowery arbours
    Cluster in the open street.

On its slopes, the Mount of Olives
    Claimed the festal joy to share;
Booths of pine and pendent willow
    Deck its ridges everywhere.*

* Neh. viii. 15; Lev. xxiii. 40.

All day long within the Temple
   Crowds there are in garments gay:
No such times of mirth and gladness
   As this anniversary.

On they march in long procession,
   Some with citrons in their hands;
Some with palm and sprigs of myrtle
   Tied with gold and silver bands.

Loud they raise their great "Hosanna,"
   High their floral emblems wave:
While a blast of silver trumpets
   Sounding clear, fresh welcome gave.*

In the night two candelabra
   In the sacred courts are set,
Lighting now the Vale of Kedron
   Now the heights of Olivet.

Every pillar, porch, and cloister
   Reddens with the fiery glow;
While the strains of hymn and Psalter
   Louder and still louder grow.

Varied sound of cymbals clashing,
   And the lurid torches' blaze,
Mingle with the choral singing,
   Till appear the morning-rays

Flashing o'er the hills of Moab.
   To this Feast the Saviour came:
Thronged the worshippers around Him
   Who had heard His Prophet-fame.

* Ps. cxviii. 24-26.

On the eighth day,* nigh the altar
   Where their hallel-hymn they sang,
Was prolonged the festal-music,
   Roused afresh each echo rang.

Then the Priest with golden goblet
   Down a rocky pathway went,
Till he reached the pool Siloam.
   Thousands thronged the steep descent.

When was filled the sacred flagon
   With the water "soft which flows;"
Loud anew outburst Hosannas,
   Loud anew the trumpet blows.

From a silver ewer he pours it
   At the brazen altar's base;
And the crowd their frondal emblems
   Yet once more triumphant raise.

Thus did speak their greatest Prophet—
   "He the day of Christ who saw":—
"From the well-spring of Salvation
   Ye with festive joy shall draw."†

Then did Jesus, Holy Saviour,
   With His loudest voice proclaim
He was both that living *Fountain*,‡
   And the true celestial *Flame*.§

---

* John viii. 37.   ‡ John vii. 37.
† Is. xii. 3.   § John viii. 12.

"I am Light of all the world—
    Brighter than the Brightest Sun:
Joyous Well-spring of Salvation,
    LIGHT, and LIFE, and LOVE, in one!"

"*I am the Light of the World.*"—John viii. 12.

"*In the last day, that great day of the feast, Jesus stood and cried, saying, 'If any man thirst, let him come unto me, and drink.'*"—John vii. 37.

"*Therefore with joy shall ye draw water out of the wells of Salvation.*"—Is. xii. 3.

XXVII

[*Bethany. Martha, Mary, and Lazarus. Lazarus is sick. The message sent across Jordan to distant Peræa. The mysterious delay of Jesus.*]

A loved and loving brother is
Laid on his couch about to die:
The darkest of all darkening clouds
Broods o'er the Home of Bethany.*

One mighty arm and one alone,
Full well the mourning sisters know,
Can in the crisis interpose
And save the desolating blow.†

Some friendly messengers are sent
Down the deep gorge with headlong speed,
They hasten to Bethabara
With the great Lord to intercede.

The urgent tidings they have brought
With beaded drops upon their brow:—
"He whom Thou lovest, Lord, is sick,
Haste to his couch! Alone canst Thou

* John xi. 1. † John xi. 22.

"Arrest in time the fleeting breath
And stay the spirit's arrowy flight,
Forbid his eyes in death to close
And bring him back to life and light;

"To the pale cheek the bloom restore,
The lustre to the dimming eye:—
Pause not; but haste Thy blessëd steps
To the swept home of Bethany."*

. . . . . .

They feel assured they have not pled
In vain. No moment will be lost
Ere the Peræan hills are left
And the deep fords of Arnon crossed.

. . . . . .

But strange! the Master lingers, when
The tide of life is ebbing fast;
When mortal shades enshroud the brow,
And soon all gleams of hope are past.†

Why these unheard, unanswered quests?
That longed-for succour, why so late?
Leaving the stricken ones alone,
Their hearts and household desolate!

[*The sisters utter their repeated dirge of sorrow.*]

Why absent, Lord, when longed for near?
The help withheld ofttimes supplied
In former days? "Hadst Thou been here
Thy friend, our brother, had not died."‡

---

* John xi. 3.   † John xi. 6.   ‡ John xi. 21–32.

They gathered weeping round the bier:
And with their plaintive refrain cried—
"Lord, if Thou only hadst been here
Our brother never should have died."

The leaves of early spring are sere,
Before the autumn winds have sighed.
"O, Lord, Thou surely wert not here,
Else he would not so soon have died."

Why cause to us one needless tear?
No former quests were thus denied;
From Thy delay in hastening here—
The pride of heart and home has died.

. . . . . .

Hush! mourning sisters, cease to weep;
The Master will true vigil keep
Over thy loved one's slumber deep,
"He only taketh rest in sleep!"

. . . . . .

Jesus is seen approaching by the Jericho road.]

At last the gladsome tidings reach,
The Lord and Master draweth nigh!
He comes! He comes! their hearts to heal—
The broken hearts of Bethany.*

The stronger-minded sister first
Rushes outside its groves of palm :—
A suppliant at her Master's feet,
For, better than all Gilead-balm,†

---

* John xi. 20.   † John xi. 20.

She hears these glorious living words
That ring out like a silver chime;
Bright messages of joy and hope
That echo to the end of time:—

"The Resurrection and the Life:"
"He that believes shall never die!"
O vanquished death, where now thy sting?
And where, O grave, thy victory?*

Within the shadowed homestead, still,
Sits Mary, brooding o'er her fears;
Their brother *gone!* she only can
In pensive silence nurse her tears.†

At last they meet! In solemn awe,
With the expectant crowd they stand
Round the sepulchral cave. They wait
To hear the gracious Lord's command.‡

Around them are the caverned vaults
Where mute unconscious sleepers lie:
Upon the one most dear has death
Stamped his impressive mockery.

Now musing on the treasured past,
Now gazing on the voiceless crypt.
Lo! they are both arrested, by
Strange sudden tears, for "*Jesus wept!*"§

O sympathetic tribute borne!
The tears of man,—the tears of God!

* John xi. 25, 26.   ‡ John xi. 38.
† John xi. 20.   § John xi. 34, 35.

In all this Gospel Idyll mark
Its holiest, tenderest episode!

Hark! o'er the silent grotto-tomb
They hear the music of His voice,
The summons—"Lazarus, come forth!"
In trembling transport they rejoice.*

That fiat of Almighty power
Has summoned back the shrouded dead.
The grave-clothes drop! and to his home
The vanished brother back is led.†

That hallowed haunt of friendship, which
Had its best inmate "lost awhile,"
Welcomes again his living tones
And is relighted with his smile.

Faith joyous folds her dove-like wings:
The weary waiting time is o'er.
Problems unsolved are solved at last,
The cloud without the bow no more!

. . . . . .

And so He often "lingers" still,
And seems to mock confiding trust,
As if resolved to thwart our will
And turn life's treasures into dust.

Hush, hush! our cherished Lazarus may
Seem bowing to the final stroke.
We rain our tears, and wildly pray—
The fleeting breath, O Lord, revoke!

* John xi. 43. † John xi. 44.

Be still; amid unanswered prayers
And baffled hopes and starless night,
Hope thou in God! At unawares
He will put adverse dealings right.

Averting oft the awful hush
Of silence. He forbids to blanch
The wasted features—stays the rush
Of Death's descending avalanche.

Or if He fail relief to send;
If called bereavement's path to tread,
To mourn with yearning hearts a friend,
A fond and fondled brother *dead!*—

It is an early summons given
To life immortal in the skies;
Another saint is sent to Heaven,
The better land to colonize!

Henceforth I trust His tarrying love,
In darkest dealings I shall rest;
Wait His own answer from above,
Assured His way is always best.

I look no more to sense and sight,
His will is mine whate'er it be:
I own, combined, His love and might,
"HE *rules the raging of the sea!*"

"WHEN THE WAVES THEREOF ARISE THOU STILLEST THEM."

"SAID I NOT UNTO THEE THAT IF THOU WOULDEST BELIEVE THOU SHOULDEST SEE THE GLORY OF GOD."

XXVIII

[*Scene: Christ passing through Jericho on His way to Jerusalem by the Valley of Achor. Zaccheus, the tax-gatherer, is numbered among His followers.*]

Jesus through the gates was passing,
  (In the flush of evening calm)
Of the oft-rebuilded city
  With its groves of fragrant balm;

When Zaccheus, small of stature,
  Who had never once before
Met the far-famed Jewish Prophet,
  Climbs a wayside sycamore;

There to see this only Teacher
  Who refused to share the hate
For the class which all the nation
  Never failed to execrate.*

In life's retrospect, that moment,
  Phantom visions seem to rise,
Grasping dealings, mean extortions,
  Haunting shapes of avarice.

* Luke xix. 2, 3, 4.

VIEW FROM THE MOUNT OF OLIVES.

(To face p. 80.)

Would the Lord one look of favour
    Cast? His sordid deeds condone?
Or, still leave him to be reaper
    Of the seed which he had sown?

Christ descries him through the branches,
    Calls him from the leafy height;
Soon the publican descending
    Owns the Saviour's love and might.*

"Son of Man!" the Master tells him,
    Came lost sinners to redeem.
"SON OF MAN!" a nature *human*,
    What that name to him must seem! †

"Son of Man," not "Son of Nation,"
    Bound by narrow sect or space.
"Son of Man!" a *world's* salvation,
    Friend and Brother of the race!

Then Zaccheus, all time coming,
    Mourning past dishonest gains,
Of his heart makes full surrender,
    And the life that still remains. ‡

Doomed no longer in his blindness
    Through the deepening shades to grope,
Conquered by redeeming kindness,
    "Achor is a door of hope!"§

Let all those who, conscience-wounded,
    Gospel peace have failed to know;
Heart and hope take from this latest
    "Memory of Jericho."

---

* Luke xix. 5, 6.   † Luke xix. 10.   ‡ Luke xix. 6–10.
    § Hosea ii. 15.

XXIX

[*Scene: Eve of the Jewish Sabbath. Bethany, the Box of precious nard. The Triumphal entrance, next day, to Jerusalem by the Olivet road. The Hosannas on the way. The tears of Jesus over against the Temple. The children's voices. Nearing death.*]

A longed-for day of rest has come:
He pauses at the cherished home,
   Before His tragic hour:
Crowds from the City flock to see
His risen friend of Bethany,
   The trophy of His power.*

Within that ever-loved retreat
Sits Mary, pensive at His feet,
   Her eyes suffused with tears;
For He has given back to her
Her Brother, Friend, and Comforter,
   Allaying all her fears.

Remembering what He is, and was,
She breaks her Alabaster Vase—
   Filled with its ointment sweet:

* John xii. 1–9.

The great Redeemer understood
The tribute of her gratitude
   Thus poured upon His feet.*

He knew, in darkening hours at hand,
With failing friends and traitor-band,
   How oft He would recall,
How she with loving thought did care
These costly spices to prepare—
   "She did it for my burial." †

. . .

Reviving Nature now is seen
Clad in its springtide robe of green;
   While hour by hour increased
The crowd of Pilgrims from afar,
Led by the light of moon and star
   Up to the holy feast. ‡

Amid the caravans which met
By the descent of Olivet,
   The Saviour rode along.
His regal entry thus He makes.
At each familiar turn there wakes
   The voice of festal song. §

Their garments on the way were spread:
They cut down branches overhead:
   Each lip is tuned to sing.

---

* John xii. 3; Matt. xxvi. 10–13.   † John xii. 7.
‡ John xii. 12.   § John xii. 13

As the meek Hero passes by
United voices raise the cry—
   "Hosanna to our King!"*

Hosanna! let Him be adored,
The Prince of Peace, Immanuel, Lord:
   Float on ye waves of sound!
Hosanna! with united breath
Hail Him as Victor over Death,
   Whose chains He hath unbound. †

If there were silence in the crowd
The very stones would cry aloud!
   It rises far and nigh—
Hosanna! every echo wakes,
From mountain slope and ferny brakes
   Hosanna! is the cry! ‡

Still onward rolls the great acclaim,
Youth, manhood, age, repeat the same:
   Ten thousand bow the knee:
Hosanna! louder shouts ascend:
The Paschal strains of Hallel blend
   In the great Jubilee.

No warrior steeds by Him are reined:
No chariot is with bloodshed stained,
   No battle-axe or spear.
No captives bound, no dismal wail,
No cheeks of tender woman pale
   Proclaim a Conqueror near.

* Mark xi. 8, 9.   † Luke xix. 37, 38; Mal. xxi. 9.
‡ Luke xix. 40.

Around Him, those His touch has healed,
The blind whose eyes He has unsealed,
   The hungry He has fed.
Widow and orphan, too, are there,
The sick ones who have claimed His care,
   And the restorëd dead.*

Hosanna! still, like distant roar—
The thunder breaking on the shore—
   Of many waters is:
As rank on rank they move along
Till they confront with holy song
   God's own metropolis. †

The earth could boast no other scene
So glorious as this radiant Queen,
   To whom profuse was given
Gigantic fortresses and towers,
The walls festooned with beauteous flowers
   Set in the azure heaven! ‡

The pillared Temple, white as snow,
The Kedron murmuring below
   Bathed in the noontide beams.
A regal cincture, gem on gem:
Like gleaming crown or diadem
   The splendid vision seems.§

  .   .   .   .

But all at once the picture fades.
The gilded roofs and colonnades
   No longer fill His eyes

---

* Matt. xxi. 14; John xii. 17, 18.   † Matt. xxi. 9, 10.
‡ Ps. lxxxvii. 3; Ps. xlviii. 2.   § Is. lxii. 3.

While gazing on that vision bright
He only sees in gloom of night
   A nation's obsequies. *

Strange in His hour of joy such grief!
Why thus in weeping seek relief?
   What tidings reach His ears?
There loomed before His eyes a trance
Of woe, too deep for utterance,
   And far transcending tears.

The towers now rising in their might
Which burst resplendent on His sight
   Would soon be girt with flame:
The ruthless foe the gates unbar,
And a wild anguish-wail from far
   His tender pity claims. †

The Saviour weeps,—He weeps aloud,
And heedless of the festive crowd
   Thinks of the fell decree
Which Zion's awful sins invoke;
While o'er her fated walls He spoke
   His dread soliloquy. ‡

"If thou hadst known in this thy day!"
But now—thy season passed away—
   I mourn thy hapless fate.
The awful crisis-hour is nigh

---

* Luke xix. 41-44.   † Matt. xxiv. 1-28.
‡ Matt. xxiii. 34-37; Luke xix. 41-45.

When thou shalt doom thy Lord to die—
"Thy house left desolate."*

. . . . . .

Still with these burning tears He pleads;
Then on once more the crowd proceeds.
   Beneath a sky serene,
On right the sacred mountain rose,
On left Moriah's rocks repose,
   The Kedron gorge between.

The Temple-Courts are reached at last.
The Golden gate of entrance past,
   New frondal tributes wave;
Some groups of loving children meet
To make the triumph-hour complete
   "He cometh us to save!" †

No music that was heard that day,
No garlands scattered on His way,
   Did truer joy afford.
They waved their tiny palms on high,
Their infant trebles swelled the cry—
   "Hosanna to the Lord!"

. . . . . .

The sun his parting radiance pours.
When end the bright and festal hours:
   Who can the scene forget?
The tones with ever-varying swell
Lingered like those of Sabbath-bell
   Upon Mount Olivet.‡

. . . . . .

---

* Matt. xxiii. 38.   † Mark xi. 11; Matt. xxi. 15, 16.
      ‡ Mark xi. 12.

Days pass; and on that solemn night
He institutes His holy rite
   Ere going forth to die.*
The Victim soon shall bow His head
The Lamb be to the slaughter led:
   And then THE VICTORY!

    * Matt. xxvi. 20, 26-30.

XXX

[*Jesus in Gethsemane. The Cup of Suffering. Submission to the Divine Will. The Angel sent to strengthen. The sleeping Disciples.*]

Three times He cried, "My Father let it pass,
This anguished cup, O let it pass from me!"
He lay convulsed upon the dewy grass
        Of lone Gethsemane.*

Now are fulfilled the words of Israel's seer,—
The slumbering sword against the Shepherd wakes : †
And the Eternal Son, beloved and dear—
        God—His own God forsakes.‡

On trembling lips the agonised refrain
Mingles with meek submission :—"But if Thou
Mayst not avert this superhuman pain—
        To Thy great will I bow.§

"Or, gracious Father! if I call aloud,
And vain be now these bitter tears and cries,
O let the time come for the rifted cloud—
        The love that never dies!"

* Matt. xxvi. 39, 42, 44.   † Zech. xiii. 7.
‡ Ps. xxii. 1 ; Luke xv. 34.   § Luke xxii. 42.

Upon the dreadful brink He stands aghast.
Beneath, the awful waves of death and sin.
Thrice He reels back affrighted. But at last
      Submissive plunges in.

The promised rainbow in the cloud appears,
Sweet chimes of love amid the surges ring,
And there is sent, to wipe His bloodstained tears,
      An Angel strengthening.*

Alas! He finds His trusted ones asleep,
Asleep when most He needed watchers kind;
"I dreamt not thus your vigils you would keep,
      And sealèd eyelids find." †

"Sleep ye on now," He adds, "and take your rest,
My night-watch of great agony is done.
These lips shall soon proclaim the tidings blest
      Of final triumph won.

"Meanwhile arise! new shades are deepening:
The Son of Man this night shall be betrayed.
With better than an Angel strengthening
      We shall not be afraid!" ‡

* Luke xxii. 43. † Mark xiv. 37-40. ‡ Mark xiv. 41, 42.

GETHSEMANE.

(*To face p.* 90.)

XXXI

[*The end approaches. Pilate and Herod. The mockery. The scourging. Crucify Him!*]

All is now ready: Come and see
The crisis-hour of His distress:
The crimson drops are on His dress
Which fell in dark Gethsemane.

In Pilate's pillared hall He waits,
With mangled face and bleeding brow.
The Roman asks Him—"Who art Thou?"
The crowd surged round the Palace gates.*

Then Herod with his men of war
Assail him with their savage jeers.
They only mock His patient tears
And leave afresh some cruel scar.†

Once more in Pilate's house He stood:
Again the unrelenting cry—
"Him crucify!" "Him crucify!"
Broke from the surging multitude.‡

* Matt. xxvii. 2-11.   † Luke xxiii. 11.   ‡ Luke xxiii. 13-24.

A reed they for a sceptre bring,
A crown of thorns surrounds His head;
In robes of mockery arrayed
They bow the knee and call Him King. *

Upon his faint and quivering frame
The lacerating scourge descends
With savage cruelty. He bends
Beneath the tragedy of shame.

The hour is come—the hour to die!
Louder the frenzied shout arose,
From the wild gathering of foes—
"HIM CRUCIFY!" "HIM CRUCIFY!"†

* John xix. 1–3.   † John xix. 15, 16.

XXXII

[*From the Prætorium to Golgotha. The procession to Calvary. The Crucifixion. The prayer for His murderers. The first offering of the Vinegar. The rejection. The silent Sufferer.*]

"*By crucifixion!*"—This the hated doom
Reserved for Jewish outcasts,—robber bands,
The brigands of Arbèla, or the thieves
That haunted the defiles of Jericho
And caves of Achor.   "The accursed death!"*
Terrific "Baptism of blood."   Exempt
Was every Roman from that basest badge
Of degradation.   Yet the sinless Christ—
The Incarnation of all goodness, He—
Divine ideal of humanity—
Is led by impious hands to undergo
Its awful shame.
    See the Great Sufferer
Led from the gates of the Prætorium
Along the tortuous street.   The noisy crowd
That dared to execrate a blameless life
Is headed by a band of soldiers; priests

* Deut. xxi. 23; Phil. ii. 8.

And rulers follow. In the centre walks
With the calm majesty of innocence
The Christ of Nazareth. A cross of wood
Sawn from some terebinth or sycamore,
On which ere long in torture He is nailed,
Is borne on shoulders wearing still the trace
Of cruel flagellation : while, beyond
All outward marks of lacerating scourge,
Linger the night-watch memories :—the hours
Of superhuman anguish : when, withdrawn
Within the shades of Olivet, He bore
The burden of a world !
                           Where now the shouts
Which but five days before had stirred the air
With loud Hosannas? Where the festive throng
With the green palms that waved triumphantly,
Or other branches carpeting the way?
They lie unheeded,—withered in the heat
Of glaring sun,—perchance made provender
For the unconscious animals which bore
Their owners to the feast. O fitful hearts !
To-day, the shout of loyal welcome rose.
To-morrow, the fierce cry of "Crucify !"

Though the great Son of God, yet was He too
"The Son of Man." His was a Holy Soul
Linked to a body exquisitely strung :
Responsive to each throb of cruel pain :—
His every nerve a chord of anguish keen.
So, after all the tortures meekly borne,
The stripes and scourgings and long agony
Of previous hours, He staggers underneath,
With dizzy brain, and feeble, tottering step

The wooden beam. Exhausted nature droops.*
No helping hand is nigh! All shrink aghast
From nearer contact with the badge of death.
That hideous log! The Roman soldiers deemed
Its touch pollution. Can they not impress
Some passing slave or mercenary Jew
To do the service they themselves disdain:
Prop up the falling Victim, and prolong
The pulses that are ebbing fast? They dread
Lest He succumb to death, before the place
Of suffering is reached—"the Hill of doom,"
And sheer exhaustion rob them of the hope
Of glutting savage eyes, by gazing on
The sight of writhing limb, and cruel nails
Transfixing hand and feet. They seize at last
On Simon, a Cyrenian, whose sons
Became in time disciples of the Lord:†
Their mother, too, one of the honoured names
Of after years—inscribed upon the roll
Of true devoted followers.‡ They compel
This sable African to bear the cross,§
Which, from that hour, he it is said has made
The symbol of his faith and reverent trust.
  On the Great Sufferer walks: while flouts and jeers
Resound along the "Dolorous Way." Precedes
A Roman herald: and with trumpet-blare
Proclaims the crime for which the Victim pays
The penalty of death. Denied is He
The sympathy to which He long had clung

---

* John xix. 17.   † Mark xv. 21.   ‡ Rom. xvi. 13.
§ Luke xxiii. 26.

With fond tenacity. Disciples all
Forsake, and flee, and cower in base despair—
A recreant band when most their trusted love
Was needed.*   His arrested ear at length
Hears kindred voices break the spell of woe.
Behind, He listens to the anguished sobs
Of weeping females: faithful from the first,
Now faithful to the last:—those upon whom
Doubtless, in days gone by, He lavished had
His tenderest compassion. Looking round
He says—" Ye daughters of Jerusalem!
Weep not for Me; but rather for yourselves
And for your children keep these anguished tears.
I ask no vengeance on the hapless ones
That doomed the Innocent. But righteous Heaven
Will not withhold the awful recompense
For this black crime of crimes. *"If these things be
Done in the green tree: what then in the dry?"* †

. . . . . .

Outside the city walls, perchance where now
Nigh to the grotto that tradition makes
The refuge of the weeping seer: a mound
Of skull-like shape identifies the site
With gloomy Golgotha. ‡ Conspicuous is
The place from every side. One pilgrim crowd
Pass up the valley of Jehoshaphat:
Another living wave comes surging down
From central Ephraim and Samaria.
With gaze transfixed they see the dying Christ,

---

* Matt. xxvi. 56.   † Luke xxiii. 27–32.   ‡ John xix. 17.

His arms outstretched, as if He would embrace
The world which had disowned Him: while the sun
Beats pitiless on His unsheltered head,
Or else in gloomy sackcloth is attired:
As if to hide himself in very shame
From witnessing the dying agonies
Of his Divine Creator!*
      Jesus speaks.
'Tis the first utterance from parchëd lips.
Ofttimes are others in that awful hour
Heard, amid blasphemies untold, to curse
The hands that nailed them to the bitter cross.
How different with Him! Alone ascends
A prayer for his own murderers. He cries—
" Father, forgive! They know not what they do." †

. . . .

The tragedy proceeds. One pause alone
Breaks the monotony of suffering :—
One struggling ray in darkness. Drops of myrrh
Mingled with vinegar, to dull the sense
Of racking pain, were offered Him to drink!
The solitary touch of pity met
With no response. He put it to His lips
Simply to taste. And then the anodyne
In silence was refused. He would accept
No mitigation in that awful hour:
Resolved to drink the chalice to its dregs. ‡
The ruffian crowd below with cruel jeer
Mocked at His tortures. Soldiers, scribes, and priests,
Vied in their insults, loudly challenging

* Jeremy Taylor.   † Luke xxiii. 34.   ‡ Mark xv. 23.

"If Thou Messiah be, then straightway come
Down from the cross, and so we shall believe.
He who saved others cannot save Himself."*
He answered not.   No word reclaiming rose
From those meek lips.   The Holy Lamb of God
Was dumb before His shearers. †   Taunted, scorned,
He bowed beneath the mystery of woe!
Calm stands the Rock of Ages, mid the surge
Of hellish passion, His the high behest—
"I come alone to do Thy will, O God." ‡

* Mark xv. 31, 32.   † Is. liii. 7.   ‡ Ps. xl. 8.

XXXIII

[*Two thieves crucified with Him, the one on the right hand, the other on the left. Supposed appeal of the Penitent thief to the Impenitent.*]*

[*Penitent Thief—*]

Why mockest thou this dying Man of God, †
His guiltless life-blood crimsoning the sod?
What gracious thought within His bosom stirs,
That prompts the pleading for His murderers?
May we not, wretched felons, share it too—
      "*Father, forgive them !*
        They know not what they do." ‡

What! railing still against that Holy One?
We justly suffer. But the Christ hath done
Nothing amiss.§ Steeped though we be in crime,
May we not listen to His words sublime:
Take to ourselves the prayer so strangely new—
      "*Father, forgive them !*
        They know not what they do."

Methought no voice of pardon was for me,
No place of safety whither I could flee.

---

* Mark xv. 27, 28; Luke xxiii. 33.   ‡ Luke xxiii. 34.
† Luke xxiii. 39, 40.   § Luke xxiii. 40, 41.

I deemed my flagrant guiltiness too great;
All hope was gone: I sank disconsolate.
I heard—what seemed too gracious to be true—
    "*Father, forgive them!*
      They know not what they do."

He spake to God as "*Father.*" Once that name
Was lisped by me with reverence: ere shame
Forbade its utterance; and I had yet
No robber haunt at far Gennesaret.
Its magic charm in happier days I knew—
    "FATHER, *forgive them!*
      They know not what they do."

I have done evil—countless sins arise
In a l their ghastliness before mine eyes.
Oft have my hands with human blood been stained,
Earth has been wronged and Heaven has been profaned.*
Still may the prayer be said for me and you—
    "*Father, forgive them!*
      They know not what they do."

I too was privileged His face to see.
I heard His words in distant Galilee.
Their music lingered in my rocky cave—
"*Those that are lost I came to seek and save.*" †
His tones of pity greet my ears anew—
    "*Father, forgive them!*
      They know not what they do."

---

* Luke xxiii, 41.   † Matt. xviii. 11.

Except for Him, of peace I could not dream,
With impious thoughts I dared the Great Supreme.
Nor God, nor man, I ever sought to please ;
Outcast, despairing, vile,—no words but these
Could ever guilty memories undo—
      " Father, forgive them !
         They know not what they do."

I prayed the prayer—" O, Lord, remember me,
When death has severed between me and Thee." *
Swift came the answer, "Verily I say
Thou shalt me find in Paradise to-day !" †
O welcome words with that glad Heaven in view—
      " Father, forgive them !
         They know not what they do."

If He hath told of pardoning mercy great
To crucifiers, base and reprobate :—
A message of salvation full and free :
O if for them—why not for you and me?
Grasp firm His death-prayer for the murderous crew—
      " Father, forgive them !
         They know not what they do."

These racking tortures will not be in vain
Which close this cruel tragedy of pain,
If, ere the final sleep, you hear His voice,
Confess your guilt, repent, believe, rejoice !
Take His last pleading as if meant for you—
      " Father, forgive them !
         They know not what they do."

    * Luke xxiii. 42.   † Luke xxiii. 43.

[*The thief on the left hand dies impenitent. The Penitent thief, the first trophy of Redeeming love, ascends with His Lord.*]

Death ends at last His agony: He is
The chartered citizen of Paradise.
The dying Jesus for the saved one waits.
Together as they reach the Heavenly gates,
Above, the golden words still gleam in view—
  "*Father, forgive them!*
   They know not what they do."

.   .   .   .

Whoe'er thou art make the same comfort thine,
Which rose of old to Heaven from lips divine;
Blest accents, uttered with His parting breath,
When rising far above the death of death,
He pled for all the world—for me, for *you*—
  "*Father, forgive them!*
   They know not what they do."

XXXIV

[*Women gathered at the Cross. Jesus commends His mother to St. John. They go together to the Beloved Disciple's home.*]

  A female band around the cross
  With tears bewail their tragic loss—
    All that the Christ had been :
  His mother, Mary, standeth by ;
  Some from the Lakeside too are nigh,
    With Mary Magdalene.*

  The dearest there attracts His eye.
  He hears her groan of agony :
    It thrills His throbbing heart :
  She looks upon her bleeding Son ;
  And thinks of all that He has done
    For her ! Can she impart

  Some human solace in that trance
  Of direst woe ? one loving glance
    Ere He has sunk in death ?
  A glance before the shadows fall
  That might the sunny hours recall
    Of holy Nazareth ?

     * John xix. 25.

The days when in His early prime
He roamed in spring or summer time
    Upon its heathy hills:
Loving their purple slopes to mount:
Or at the mossy village fount
    The homely pitcher fills?

As, with life's pulses ebbing fast,
A dying look around He casts,
    A "friend" His eyes arrest:
The cherished of the chosen three,
The honoured Son of Zebedee,
    Who leaned upon His breast.

Amid augmenting pangs severe,
When torturing nail and cruel spear
    His Holy flesh has riven;
With pleading look and eye-ball dim,
He turns with yearning soul to him.
    A sacred trust is given!

The favour asked is quickly done:
"Woman, behold thy Son:"—and "Son
    Behold thy Mother!"* He
Desired she might be spared the sight,—
The gloom of ever-deepening night
    Which closed the agony.

Once more she marks the ghastly trace
Of stripe and scourge, the pallid face,
    Then takes a last farewell.

    * John xix. 27.

By John's strong hand and heart upheld,
Her tide of surging grief is quelled,
    She goes with him to dwell.*

Onward they pass from street to street:
They reach the Home with trembling feet,
    Mid crowds that throng the way.
The blood of Paschal offering shed
Was still upon its lintels, red,
    Besprinkled yesterday.

    * John xix. 27,

XXXV

[" *Eloi, Eloi, lama sabachthani.*" " *It is finished.*" *The crowd disperse to their homes.*]

When a thick darkness brooded o'er the scene,
And like a curtain palled the heavens serene;
When earthquake tremors shook the solid ground,
And mystic portents filled the air around :
The plaint rose piteous from the shameful tree—
" *Why, O my God, hast Thou forsaken me?*"

'Tis not the spear-gash and the streaming blood,
Nor cry of vengeance from the multitude,
'Tis not the thorns that pierce the mangled brow,
My God! my God and Father! it is THOU!
Forgive the loud appeal I make to Thee,—
   And tell me, " *Why hast Thou forsaken me?*"

Our sins, our sins, upon the Cross He bare :
With man's worst tortures far beyond compare.
His Father's face is veiled in dire eclipse,
The cup of wrath is drained with quivering lips.
Climax of suffering—severance from THEE!
" *My God! my God! Thou hast forsaken me!*"

Yet, not forsaken !—Soon is heard the cry,
"'*Tis finished!*"—pledge of final victory.

A peace divine returns before He dies,
Light, long withdrawn, suffused His closing eyes.*
Joyful once more, His father's face to see,
He cries—"*My God has* NOT *forsaken me!*"

. . . .

Silent scene of love and wonder!
Sealëd tombs are rent asunder,
Quaketh too the slumbering sod.
While the crowd, their bosoms beating,
Homewards go with awe repeating—
"THIS MAN TRULY WAS THE SON OF GOD!"†

* Ps. xxii. 21, 22.   † Matt. xxvii. 54.

XXXVI

[A personal history. Mary Magdalene, out of whom Christ cast seven devils. Her devotion to the Saviour during His ministry: specially at the close. A watcher by the Cross, and the herald of His Resurrection.]

Her name, like pensive star serene,
Shines radiant in the gospel sky:
It still survives, it cannot die—
Thrice-honoured Mary Magdalene.

Once on her early life there fell
The shadow of a dread disease,
No mortal power could soothe, to ease
Or save her from its demon-spell.

At last drew near the Prince of Life,
He listened to her anxious quest;
He rocked the fiendish waves to rest,
Changed into peace infernal strife.*

Henceforth, for all her future years,
She gave to Him the soul restored,
Owned Him her Heavenly Lord adored,
And served with duteous love and tears.†

* Luke viii. 1, 2.   † Luke viii. 3.

When the impending crisis came,
The hour and power of darkness deep,
She did her holiest vigils keep;
Devotion lit its brightest flame.

The cross she trembling lingers nigh,
Watches His eyelids closing dim,
And gilds the black horizon-rim
Of superhuman agony.*

When all was over,—when His sun
Had set in terror and in blood,
Still the devoted watcher stood,
No task of love was left undone.

Fails that tremendous day of dread
To blanch her cheek with *selfish* fears,
Amid an agony of tears
Her only thought is for the Dead.†

. . . . .

Nature is mute—no zephyrs stir
The dawn of that first Easter morn,
When weeping, trembling, sad, forlorn,
She stands before the Sepulchre.

But lo! displaced has been the stone,
It has been rolled away by night;
She, panic-stricken at the sight,
Gazes bewildered and alone.‡

---

* Matt. xxvii. 55, 56.
† Matt. xxviii. 1; Luke xxiii. 55, 56; Luke xxiv. 1.
‡ Matt. xxviii. 2, 3, 4; John xx. 1.

The One on earth she cleaved to most,
Whose pallid face she hoped to see
And bathe in tears:—had suddenly
To her adoring eyes been lost.

. . . . . .

"My loving Lord they've ta'en away,"
In bitterness of soul she said,
"I know not where He has been laid!"*

. . . . . .

And now it is the break of day.

Ah! bitter is the thought to her,
Standing outside the vacant tomb,
As darkening shades have ceased to loom:
That the well-guarded sepulchre—

With hands profane had rifled been.
No vigil now but of despair.
The Christ!—the Christ! He is not there;
She gazes wildly on the scene.

Meanwhile, an angel bright appears,
Where the loved Lord was lately laid,
"Woman! why weepest thou?" he said,†
"Cease thy despair and dry thy tears."‡

Another Voice and Form is nigh,
The angel's words are heard again.
Arrested by the strange refrain,
She turns her round to make reply.§

* John xx. 13. ‡ Mark xvi. 5, 6.
† Matt. xxviii. 5, 6. § John xx. 14, 15.

"MARY!"—the name pronounced:—Can this
Be but a fevered dream of night?
Some vision vain that mocks her sight
And only leaves her comfortless?*

"RABBONI!" "Master!" straight she cries,†
"At Thy dear feet I trembling fall.
O more than glad return, for all
My poor but faithful ministries."

. . . . . .

"Last at the cross, first at the tomb"—
The honoured one who earliest heard
The tidings of a risen Lord:
And bore them thence to Christendom! ‡

* John xx. 15, 16.   † John xx. 16.
§ John xx. 18; Luke xxiv. 10.

XXXVII

[*Scene: South-west of Jerusalem. Two disciples on the way to Emmaus. Jesus joins them. He breaks bread with them at their evening meal, and vanishes out of sight.*]

[*First disciple to his fellow.*]

Are our hopes for ever blighted,—
    Dashed in pieces to the ground?
Are we left like men benighted,—
    Only a deceiver found?

All most loved must we surrender,
    As the leaves of autumn fall;
Deem our Master a Pretender,
    Who had never loved at all?

Are the many deeds of kindness
    False, His hands of mercy wrought,
Healing sickness—curing blindness—
    Giving life! Can all be nought?*

[*Second disciple.*]

Yes, alas, my hopes must languish,
    For these eyes with horror saw

* Luke xxiv. 13-18.

Him I clung to, die in anguish
On the heights of Golgotha.

. . . . .

[*Here a stranger approaches, and joins in the converse.*]

What are these musings burdening your hearts?
What means this sorrow and disquietude,
Which turns your festal joy to grief and tears?*

[*They answer.*]

Dost thou not know that dread events
   Have here transacted been?
Died has the Christ, mid wild portents
   Nigh Kedron's dark ravine. †

The Christ to whom our hearts had clung—
   The Holy Son of God,
On an accursëd cross has hung
   And shed His guiltless blood.

We fondly trusted that He came
   The promise to fulfil;
And in His Heavenly Father's name
   Redeemëd Israël. ‡

Now in the silent tomb He lies,
   Victim of cruel fate;
With Him the hope of ages dies;
   We are disconsolate!

---

* Luke xxiv. 17.   † Luke xxiv. 18–20.
‡ Luke xxiv. 21.

That He indeed at morn appeared
To certain women, it is said;
A rumour vague, the worst is feared:
We mourn uncomforted.*

. . . . .

[*The stranger was Jesus. He drew near and went
with them. But their eyes were holden, that they should
not know Him.*]

He does not wonder that their sanguine thoughts
Have vanished with His death. They falsely dreamt
The great Messiah-Saviour would appear
Crowned, not with thorns, but golden diadem
Circling His brow; begirt with conqueror's sword
And holding regal sceptre; with acclaims
From a united Israel! Foolish ones,
And slow of heart, to misinterpret thus
The teachings of their prophets; who foretold
Their coming King, not charioted in pomp
And outward splendour: but as pre-ordained
To shed His blood a sacrifice for sin—
"A man of sorrows, and acquaint with grief;"
Despised, rejected, crucified, and slain:—
The sword of Heaven awaking from its sheath
To smite the Shepherd! Ought not, surely, Christ
"To suffer these things?"—pay that awful debt
That He might save a lost and ruined race:—
"Made sin for them, although He knew no sin?" †

The cross, the cross, with all its bitter shame
Was thus revealed to two misgiving hearts

* Luke xxiv. 22-24.   † Luke xxiv. 25, 26.

As a divine *necessity.* New light
Was poured upon these memorable hours,
Piercing their shroud of awe and mystery!

. . . .

In eager converse they pursue their way.
Engrossed with sadder themes, they little note
What otherwise had made its mute appeal,—
The teeming wealth of Nature, all around
In that her loveliest season. Lingering group
Along the road, of Paschal Pilgrims, caught
Fresh inspiration from the varied hues
Of plain and mountain: from the budding vines
And verdant fig-trees—trills of sweetest sound
Wafted from every copse. They pause at last
And at the threshold of some humble door
Invite the stranger who their hearts had won
To be their guest. Desirous to prolong
The musings by the way, which had revived
Their faltering hopes:—"Abide with us," they said,
"For it is toward evening, and the day
Is well-nigh spent." Consenting, He went in
To tarry with them.* Then the closing meal
Is soon made ready; and the talk proceeds
Till the night-shadows have begun to fall.
Some loaves of the unleavened Paschal-bread
Still had a place upon the homely board.
He blessed and brake them. But in doing so,
(Perchance they spied the wound-prints on His hands,
Or recognised the old familiar voice)—
He vanished in a moment out of sight.†

* Luke xxiv. 28, 29.   † Luke xxiv. 31.

The seat was vacant which had just been filled
By the great Master,—*Christ has risen indeed!*
Their eyes, once more, have seen the living Lord
They love! In trembling transport they exclaim—

"Did not our hearts within us burn
As at our side He gently spake!
Let us speed back ere morning break
And tell abroad His glad return."*

Soon do they haste along the way,
No longer nursing thoughts of sorrow;
Long ere the dawning of the morrow,
While lingered yet the light of day—

They reach Jerusalem; and find
The watchers of the Holy Tomb
With others in an upper room.†
  Lo! all at once, with accents kind,

The Lord Himself is standing by:
They gaze alike with joy and wonder
Upon death's fetters rent asunder
The grave exchanged for Victory!‡

"Why are ye troubled, thus?" He said,
"And why with doubts my presence greet?"
He showed to them His hands and feet:
Their quailing hearts were comforted.§

No longer have they tears to weep:
The word of "Peace" so well they know,

* Luke xxiv. 32.   ‡ Luke xxiv. 36.
† Luke xxiv. 33-35. § Luke xxiv. 39-42.

Lulls every fear to rest: and so
" He giveth His belovëd sleep." *

"Go!" was His farewell word to them,
And preach repentance in My Name.
To all, *the risen Christ* proclaim, †
   " BEGINNING AT JERUSALEM!"

 * Luke xxiv. 36 ; John xx. 19, 20.
  † Luke xxiv. 46, 47.

XXXVIII

[*A group of desponding fishermen. Scene: Evening on the beach of Bethsaida. Simon, son of Jonas, carrying a fisher's coat, is the speaker. He abandons hope and proposes to return to his own calling: "I go a-fishing."*]

Brothers, have our dreams all perished,
    Hallowed visions of the past!
Have the thoughts we fondly cherished
    Been too beautiful to last?
Must we bury now with sorrow
    Golden hopes of golden years:
Dreading that each coming morrow,
    Only will confirm our fears?
        "I go a-fishing." *

Take the night-boat from the shallows,
    Trim the sail and launch the net,
Let us to our former calling
    On our own Gennesaret.
I had dreamt far other ending
    To these three most blissful years,
But, if hope must be surrendered,
    Then, through breaking heart and tears,
        "I go a-fishing."

* John xxi. 3.

Long they plunge amid the darkness,
    Slow the shades of night withdraw,
Till the sun in regal splendour
    Climbs the heights of Gadara.
Vain have been their midnight labours,
    Hours are spent in fruitless toil,
Morn has come, and yet has brought them
    No reward of gleaming spoil—
        Caught they nothing.*

.   .   .   .

Who is this? A lonely stranger,
    Speaking from the shell-strewn shore,†
"Cast your net and ye shall find them."
    Lo! at once a wondrous store!‡
"'Tis the Lord! the Risen Jesus;
    'Tis our Master, hear His voice!"§
In the rapture of the moment
    They believe, adore, rejoice!
        Ends their night-watch.

Once before the net had failed them,‖
    But this wondrous final "take"
On the beach at morn was landed:
    Not a mesh was found to break.
Parable to all true toilers
    (Midnight strain and baffled oar)—
Safe at last, their freight immortal
    Brought is to the heavenly shore:
        Nets unbroken.¶

* John xxi. 3.   § John xxi. 7.
† John xxi. 4.   ‖ Luke v. 6.
‡ John xxi. 6.   ¶ John xxi. 11.

Best of all, their Lord is with them!
He, the Conqueror of death,
Stands once more amid the memories
Of His favoured "Chinnereth,"
Hearkening to its music-ripples
Breaking on the silver sand,
Holding, in the hush of day-dawn,
With the loved apostle-band
Blessëd converse!

. . . . . .

"A fire of coals, fish laid thereon and bread:"*
By unseen hands this lowly meal is spread.
Pledge of meeting,
Joyous greeting,
In the cloudless morn above,
At His Feast of endless love! †

"Weeping may endure for a night, but joy cometh in the morning."—Ps. xxx. 5.

"I will come again, and receive you unto Myself; that where I am, there ye may be also."—John xiv. 3.

* John xxi. 9. † John xxi. 9-14.

XXXIX

[Scene: Bethany. The Ascension. The disciples return to Jerusalem.]

Of all the hallowed haunts there be
Nestling beneath the Syrian sky,
More lovely none the eye can see
Than consecrated BETHANY.

It was the favoured home of Christ,
Shrouded in olive, fig, and vine,
And there three loving hearts sufficed
To cheer His human soul divine.

At dewy eve, when pressed with care
And spirit weary:—often thus
He climbed the mountain-path, to share
The holy home of Lazarus.

Leaving the world He died to save,
And ready to ascend on high,
He would that Bethany might have
His last and closing memory.

. . . . . .

Angels the Golden Gates unbar,
A cloud receives Him out of sight:
Lost from their gaze, like morning star,
Amid a blaze of Heavenly light.

The orphan'd band, with anguish moved,
Feel while they take a sad farewell,
Their "Loved and lost," their Lost and loved,
Is with them still, invisible.

Nerved with new grace and power from Heaven,
Onwards they go from land to land,
Bound by "the marching orders" given,—
Bold to fulfil their Lord's command—

> *" Go ye forth to all the world,*
>   *Teach its tribes from shore to shore:*
> *Let your banner be unfurled,*
>   *'I AM WITH YOU EVERMORE!"*

> *" Of My cross unfold the story,*
>   *To My feet fresh trophies bring:*
> *Let the watchword gleam before ye*
>   *'CONQUER AND STILL CONQUERING!'"*

"And many other signs truly did Jesus in the presence of His disciples, which are not written in this book. But these are written, that ye might believe that Jesus is the Christ, the Son of God; and that believing ye might have life through His name."

—John xx. 30, 31.

www.ingramcontent.com/pod-product-compliance
Lightning Source LLC
Chambersburg PA
CBHW030357170426
43202CB00010B/1400